curandeiro and sometimes a *feiteceiro*. In Malaya he is a *mendug*, in Borneo a *dukun* . . . among the Eskimos an *angakok*. But in all these widely separated places he is the "doctor" of the village. He is greatly feared and respected; and he is sometimes evil. . . .

As a curious and roving observer, Harry Wright has gone from the headwaters of the Maranon and the Amazon to the jungles of New Guinea and the villages of the ancient Slave Coast of Africa. He has witnessed the strange rites of the "Taro Cult" in Papua; the "Jackal dance" of the Bapende in the Belgian Congo; the weird workings of the "Vivala madness" in Dutch New Guinea; and the almost incredible evidence of extra-sensory perception and communication among the primitive peoples of these continents.

Oriented by his own scientific training, and writing from his own eye-witness experiences, Dr. Wrig' , an outstand ber of the Explorers -inating material a baffling myste   ies— occult of the prac   itioners   ncraft, , and "black magic."

WITNESS TO WITCHCRAFT

WITNESS TO WITCHCRAFT

———❦———

HARRY B. WRIGHT

41016

NEW YORK : FUNK & WAGNALLS COMPANY

1

This book is respectfully dedicated to the two men who have influenced me most deeply: The late João Alberto Lens de Barros, founder of the Fundação Brasil Central for the economic development of the Matto Grosso of Brazil; and John Alden Mason, Ph.D., of the University Museum, University of Pennsylvania.

ACKNOWLEDGMENTS

My thanks for assistance in obtaining the material in this book are extended to Orlando Vilas Boas and his two brothers, leaders of the Roncador-Xingú Expedition of Brazil; to the Australian officers of the Mandated Territory of New Guinea; to the late King Tribuvana of Nepal; to Prince Aho Glèlè of Dahomey; and to the following witch doctors: Lusungu of the Bapende; Pamantauho and Choro of South America, and Danga of New Guinea. Grateful acknowledgment is made to Theon Wright for his generous help in the preparation of this book, and to Marjorie Phillis Pearle for her invaluable editorial assistance.

HARRY B. WRIGHT

WITNESS TO WITCHCRAFT

INTRODUCTION

On March 15, 1951, Dr. H. F. Dunbar presented a paper before the College of Physicians in Philadelphia, entitled "Emotions and Bodily Change." He wrote:

"Socrates reported to his Greek countrymen that in one respect the Barbarian Thracians were in advance of civilization. They knew the body could not be cured without the mind. 'This,' he continued, 'is the reason why the cure of many diseases is unknown to the physicians of Hellas, because they are ignorant of the whole.' "

At about the same time Dr. Harry B. Wright, a Philadelphia dentist and a member of the Explorers' Club, was making his way through the tangled jungle of the Belgian Congo. He was looking for a lady witch doctor who, as things turned out, helped to prove Socrates' point.

When Harry Wright returned to Philadelphia later that year, Dr. Dunbar's paper came to his attention. The connection between Dr. Dunbar's statement and his own experiences with primitive medicine became obvious to him. The similarities between the methods of witch doctors and the techniques of modern psychology and psychiatry had already been noted by a few scientific men. Dr. Charles Pidoux, a French psychiatrist, had studied methods of mental healing practices by witch doctors in the Niger country. But these similarities are not yet widely enough recognized.

Harry Wright has always been a man of curiosity—and curiosity has few limits. The curious man, it is said, follows his nose, wherever it leads him, probing into secrets that may

1

have been lying buried for centuries. The story that follows is the record of his travels over the past dozen years when he divided his time between his Philadelphia practice, and the jungles of South America, Africa and Oceania.

It is a story of an adventure in a world of primitive medicine. It offers no scientific treatises, however, and no conclusions. It is simply a story of exploration and adventure, and behind it lies a pattern of knowledge that is as old as mankind and as new as tomorrow.

1

As we drifted slowly downriver, the banks closed in on us—high green cliffs on one side and towering trees that over-hung the jungle on the other—and filled me with a suffocating sensation of being compressed into the jungle itself. Pips was right, I thought; it has been a "fool's errand." When I left Iquitos, heading westward into the jungles of the Gran Pajonal, Pips Cato had said: "You do not even know why you are going into the country, and you certainly do not know whether you will come out alive!"

As to the latter, I was fairly sure I would come out. There were no immediate or specific dangers, beyond the constant menace of poisonous snakes and head-hunting Indians. What disturbed me was that the whole trip seemed to have become senseless. And then there was also the matter of Gabrio's toothache.

It was late in August and the hot, humid skies filled the air with an oppressive foreshadowing of the torrential rains to come. The rains that sluice down upon the Gran Pajonal

from the Andean Cordilleras, filling the immense blanket
of rotting vegetation known as the rain forest, were due any
day. There have been times when the land is covered with
a vast sheet of turgid water, with only the tops of the giant
puna trees lying like immense lily pads on the flat surface,
surrounded by floating debris and the bodies of drowned
animals.

Our dugout moved with exasperating slowness and Gabrio, my Jívaro guide, was paying more attention to his aching tooth than to the paddle. Now and then he looked at
the high-banked shore, as if he expected to see a dental
clinic in this infested land. We were heading south toward
the Upper Marañón, through the rugged Condor Mountain
range along the disputed boundary between Peru and Ecuador—possibly the least traveled country on earth, if one ex-
cepts such bleak and completely uninhabited places as the
middle of Greenland and Australia's Never-Never Land.

As a matter of fact, I did know why I went into this
country, although I would not have admitted it to Pips—
whose real name was Dr. Pereiro Cato. I had hoped to take
some pictures of Indian rituals. Since this would have been
less than no reason at all to Pips, I did not mention it to
him.

I had heard of the strange and colorful *brujos*, or witch
doctors, who could make men shrivel and die, or heal an
arm half torn from its shoulder socket by a jaguar, in a
matter of days. I am a doctor, in a specialized field; but
my curiosity was more than scientific. These ceremonies,
half-religious and half-medical, are among the most mysterious practices in the world. Early in my life, when I lived
as a boy in western Wyoming, I had visited the Cheyenne
Reservation with old Chief Robert Lame Deer and had witnessed the Peyote Cult rituals. I have never lost the intense

curiosity I then developed in the primitive practices of medicine men.

It was quite probable, as I thought at the time, that I would never again have an opportunity to see first hand these weird rites of the Huambizas and Pauté tribes of South America, some of which appeared to embody knowledge lost to the world for centuries or even thousands of years and found only among the forgotten relics of this ancient land of the Incas.

I had come as far as Iquitos on a more or less scheduled journey, intending to take some pictures and return to Belém, on the coast of Brazil, from where I would take a plane back to the United States. But certain things I had heard about the tribes, further back in the winding passageways cut by rivers through the dense primeval forests of the upper Amazon basin, made me decide to penetrate further into this more or less forbidden country.

The Indian witch doctors knew of medicines, presumably unknown to modern medical science, which would cure leprosy when chaulmoogra oil would merely arrest it. They held fantastic rites for those dying of malaria, and injected a concoction made of boiled bark into the veins with a wooden needle—and the patient would be cured within a few weeks!

My interest was centered primarily in the rites. I had fairly good camera equipment with me, and I wanted to return with some pictures that could not be duplicated. Hence my quick decision, when the chance was offered, to go upriver as far as I could with the steamboat, and then take off into the jungle on my own.

When I advised Dr. Pereiro Cato, in Iquitos, of my intentions—and invited him to join me—his swarthy face, with its bristling square beard and small moustache, was a picture of exasperation and agitation. He fairly scowled at me.

"Of course I know why I am going in," I told him. "I want to see the country!"

"Country!"

He swung his hand in an arc, as if it were a compass needle. The gesture took in the vast expanse of rain forest, stretching westward in steaming layers of green ridges, rising into the dim blue peaks of the Cordilleras, which stood like cold sentinels in the west. "You want to see *that* country? Why is it you Americans from the North insist upon being heroes for no reason? If you wish to die, there are many useful ways of doing it. Begin a revolution, or assassinate someone you do not like—in the public interest. Then you will be a useful hero. But do not go in where you will simply be a dead man and not a hero at all. Your head will become a small thing—" He made a circle of the index fingers and thumbs of both hands to indicate the anticipated dimensions of my head, once the Jívaros got through shrinking it.

"That is not to be a hero," he concluded. "It is to be a great damned fool!"

I laughed. As a matter of fact, I did not take Pips Cato's comments too seriously. I knew he enjoyed the companionship of anyone who would talk with him, and since I would talk with him, he did not want to see me leave. I was free-lancing through the country, taking pictures in a leisurely way. But when I suggested that he accompany me, he shuddered.

"It is not bad enough that you go on a fool's errand yourself," he muttered. "You must have another fool to go with you! But this one is no fool." He tapped his chest, and then suggested we have a drink.

I liked Pips Cato. He was one of those strange, nomadic

men of medicine that are often found in remote places. He was small and dapper, with a face the color of saddle leather. He wore a minute moustache and a square-cut beard that gave him a jaunty appearance. He was quite typical of back country Brazil and eastern Peru. For many years he had labored rather miscellaneously as a medical attendant for rubber hunters or nomadic gold seekers of this region. He had a thin face and a pot belly, which I suspected was due to a malignant disease of the bowels. He always wore baggy white trousers and a pith helmet, which he insisted had been given him by Lord Kitchener—although he never volunteered any explanation for the strange gift, or even the circumstances under which he might have known the great Englishman.

Since I could not persuade him to accompany me, I decided to go it alone. A small river steamboat was leaving Iquitos with a group of rubber hunters, and I arranged passage on this as far as the Morona River. From that point I hoped to make my way across country to the Pauté River and turn northward toward Zamora, which lies inside the Ecuadorean border at the foot of the Cordilleras.

The trip upriver in the steamboat was uneventful. My companions were Brazilians, and except for some polite intercourse under the strained conditions imposed by our almost total ignorance of each other's language, I had little to do with them. The small river boat stopped at a trading place below the Morona, and I left them.

From this point onward I traveled by dugout, in territory that was both lonely and treacherous. In the small settlements along the banks of the river there were usually one or two *patrones,* a garrison of a few Peruvian soldiers, and the rest were slaves, euphemistically called "children of the *patrón.*" I had intended to go up to the Marañón as far as Pongo de Manseriche, at which point the Pauté River flows

into the Upper Marañón; but I could not find anyone willing
to guide me.

By good luck, I acquired the services of Gabrio, a Jívaro of
the Huambiza tribe, and he agreed to take me into the neighboring Huambiza country. While it was reputedly less hostile than the Pauté country above, it was also less glamorous;
but I was forced to settle for what I could get. As things
turned out, what I got was practically nothing.

We ventured some distance upriver, into tributaries which
glide through dense and dangerous jungle. We stopped at
small villages; but when it was made known through Gabrio
that I sought to learn "medicine" from one of the great
brujos, I found myself regarded with suspicion, and in some
cases with visible anger.

A white man in this country obviously has no credentials.
He is lucky or unlucky depending purely upon the tribes
he happens to visit. In my case, there were no incorrigible
Chamas or Campas but only the mildly hostile Huambizas,
and I was not exposed to the fierce dangers which often
threaten the unwary traveler in this remote country. The
undying hatred of white people, born of the bitter genocidal
wars carried on first by the Spaniards and later by the Portuguese, had not ascended to the north banks of the Marañón.

The Indians had little contact with white people. The
half-caste garrison soldiers were for the most part Indian and
Negro, and they offered little more help than the natives. By
the time I turned southeastward again, heading down one of
the tributaries toward the Marañón, I was ready to confess
that Pips Cato had been right about one thing: it was a
"fool's errand." I had not even seen a witch doctor, although
there must have been several in the small villages I had
visited.

And now there was the matter of Gabrio's toothache. He

had been complaining about it for two days, and when I told him I was a tooth doctor he shook his head violently.

He was a wizened little man, with narrow shoulders, a pot belly and a disproportionately large head surmounted by a tangled mat of straight, black hair. I had purchased him, in a sense, from the patrón of the rubber camp on the Morona River; that is, I had left a small camera and some film as a "deposit" until I should return Gabrio to him. Gabrio's cheerful, grinning face and unfailing good humor had won my admiration and almost my affection, if such a sentiment can be said to exist toward a hideously painted savage whose relatives and immediate antecedents were head hunters.

In this barbarously cruel and treacherous country, a friendly face was like manna from heaven, however. Gabrio supplied not only human companionship but also the physical comforts of my existence, attending to all my wants—such as setting my hammock and arranging the mosquito netting at night; squatting in front of a small fire to watch for jaguars—or *tigres*, as they are called—and slithering ten-foot snakes; preparing stews made of well-cooked wild pig meat, tree rodents and a few feathered friends we killed in the forest.

He also supplied certain spiritual comforts; for, although we were somewhat apart in means of communication, since I could not speak much of his language and he knew only a few words of mine, we had learned to talk by signs and grunts. We had gone quite a few miles up the tributary river from the Upper Marañón, and were now headed back again; and I had learned to depend on Gabrio's knowledge of the country and the habits of the Indians to see me through safely.

Below us the wide Marañón lay like a flat yellow snake on the immense green blanket of seemingly endless jungles, draining off the concealed water from the marshes. Once I reached the Marañón I could probably make my way down-river to Iquitos again, perhaps on one of the river steamboats which infrequently traverse the river up as far as the Morona, carrying rubber hunters and their equipment.

I had asked Gabrio for information about any of the brujos he might have been acquainted with, but either he misunderstood me or professed ignorance as a result of fear. On this morning, however, the pain in his jaw seemed to out-weigh all other problems. His eyes shone feverishly under the tangled mat of black hair, and now and then he pressed his fist against his jaw and clawed at the lower lip, as if to show the source of his agony.

"Look, Gabrio," I said, with some exasperation. "Me doc-tor! Fix tooth!"

I tried, with signs and the few words of his tribal dialect that I knew, to make him understand that I could probably relieve him. He merely shook his head again, gnashing his teeth as if he would crush the offending pain in his jaw.

"White man's magic not good for Indian," he muttered. "Me see doctor."

He pronounced it "dog—eetah," something like dogeater, and after a moment of puzzlement I realized he wanted to see a witch doctor. He was pointing to the river bank, where I could see traces of an Indian village.

My time was growing short. If we did not reach Iquitos before the heavy rains, I might be held up for weeks and would miss my plane for Belém, on the East Coast, where I had a connection through to Philadelphia. Gabrio's stub-born attitude was annoying; yet I knew he could not travel with his tooth in such a condition, so there was nothing to do but put in at the village.

Gabrio quickly routed out the "dogeetah." He was a thin, emaciated old man with an expression of wisdom and craftiness, which is almost a professional trademark of witch doctors. It is hard to describe the particular qualities of this expression, which is sensed rather than seen. In succeeding years I would see these fellows perform in many places: in West Africa, Malaya and New Guinea; but this was the only time I would ever come to one with a patient seeking dental help. It seemed a bit ridiculous; yet I was aware of the complete faith Gabrio had in this man, although he was from another tribe and I doubt if Gabrio had met him before.

I began to understand why Gabrio had turned down my offer of help. It was not lack of respect for the "white man's magic." All Indians had that respect, and some of them hate white men because of the respect they have for his powers. This was something else: not lack of faith in me, but absolute, unquestioning faith in the witch doctor. This was evident in the manner of each as Gabrio chattered in his tribal dialect, making gestures and exposing a row of grimy, unsightly teeth.

The village practitioner nodded gravely; and I observed that he was also watching me. Gabrio waved in my direction once or twice, perhaps explaining that I was a "white doctor" and the old man nodded each time. There was no professional envy in his glance. It was a calculating, practical sort of appraisal.

I knew I was in for the time lost during the professional visit, and I prepared to watch with some interest the techniques to be employed. The strange ministrations of witch doctors always interested me, and this afforded a rare opportunity of witnessing the entire performance intimately. I would be able to watch the thing from a ringside seat, like a visiting surgeon observing a colleague in the arena.

As events will show, Gabrio either did not have a tooth-ache—or he had one that would have defied the best of modern dentists. As I watched Gabrio's man of medicine prepare for the practice of his queer art, I realized—possibly for the first time with any conscious perception of its importance—how completely Gabrio accepted the man's craft, with all its odd and ridiculous facets. Call it faith; or call it credulity. Whatever it was, it was a variety of what we often refer to as "psychotherapy" or the science of mental healing.

Gabrio's glittering eyes began to soften as soon as the witch doctor took over. The native practitioner was tall for his tribe, with a wrinkled, ancient visage, and sharp, knowing eyes. He paid little attention to the sanitary formalities common to the simplest medical treatment. He did not wash his hands; and from the appearance of his hands, I doubted if he had ever performed this pre-operative ceremony. There was no dental chair, of course. He merely directed Gabrio to sit on the ground, and squatted in front of him, taking Gabrio's head between his knees.

Gabrio opened his mouth, exposing a cavernous array of stained, probably infected, teeth. The local doctor shoved one grimy fist into Gabrio's mouth, holding the back of Gabrio's head with the other hand, and prying open his jaws with sheer force. Gabrio grunted, but seemed to accept this rather abrupt diagnostic intimacy in good faith. About all that was left of his face, besides his mouth, were two beady eyes that peered confidently above the bridge of his flat nose. Two probing fingers nudged around the inflamed side of his gums, and the medicine man grunted with satisfaction—although what he had learned from this rough diagnosis I could not imagine.

A boy, apparently an apprentice, brought a bowl filled with a filthy-looking liquid. The witch doctor bent over this, murmuring some kind of incantations. Meanwhile, his eyes were fixed on Gabrio with a hypnotic stare. His body swayed slightly as he murmured his "prayers."

The witch doctor suddenly reached for the bowl, swooped it to his face and gulped down the liquid. It was not at all surprising to me when he immediately retched and vomited the contents on the ground. My own professional sense, gained over years of practice, had become so numbed by the procedure thus far that I was more curious than horrified.

The witch doctor, who must have been at least sixty which is old for an Indian, waved his hand as a signal for another bowl. The bowl was brought to him, and he repeated the process. As to what was being accomplished by this internal medication—not upon the patient, but upon the person of the doctor—I could only conjecture. But there was no doubt of its outward effect upon Gabrio. Gabrio was staring with fascinated attention at the local practitioner, and the latter had assumed a rapt, almost ecstatic expression. He signalled with his hand to his assistant, and the next instant the assistant whirled Gabrio over so that he was lying on the ground, his face upward. The witch doctor kneeled above him, holding Gabrio's head firmly between his knees.

Once again he thrust his hand halfway into Gabrio's mouth; and at the same time he began to chew furiously on a tobacco-like bag he had taken into his own mouth, spitting on the ground first on one side of Gabrio, and then on the other. All the while he muttered over and over the words of the strange chant, in a weird, monotone rhythm.

The entire affair might have been amusing, had it not been for the fierce intensity of the old fellow's manner. He was going about this as seriously as any surgeon performing a critical operation.

I remained a few feet away, watching the performance with growing interest. I was not unacquainted with the basic precepts of native sorcery—particularly the need of establishing a rapport of absolute confidence between the practitioner and the patient. The complete faith with which Gabrio submitted to the Indian "doctor's" ministrations, to the intimacies inside his mouth, would have served as an object lesson in the proper relationship between patient and physician in our more civilized society.

Suddenly the witch doctor leaned forward and put his mouth against Gabrio's swollen cheek. He began to suck, furiously and noisily. The area was obviously tender, and Gabrio howled in agony; but the witch doctor continued to suck at his cheek, his assistant helping to keep Gabrio's head firmly wedged against the ground.

Finally he raised his head, and spat out something. I stepped closer and observed that it was a splinter of wood. How he had gotten it into his mouth I did not know; but I was sure it had not come through Gabrio's cheek. The old man looked around, uttering some sharp words in his native tongue, which I assumed referred to the result of his treatment.

Gabrio raised his head to stare at the offending splinter, but the old man shoved his head back on the ground again rather roughly, and resumed his sucking.

His next expectoration was a mouthful of ants. I became absorbed in the legerdemain. The old man seemed to have passed these things unobserved into his mouth; and when the third spitting produced a grasshopper, and the fourth a lizard, I became more than curious. The lizard was the *pièce de résistance.* He dangled it proudly by the tail, showing it to the other Indians who crowded around the pair.

Gabrio was permitted to sit up, and the medicine man appeared to question him as to how he felt, with these offending objects out of his teeth. Gabrio felt rather gingerly of his cheek, and nodded; but from his expression and the few words I understood, I gathered that the tooth still ached.

At this point the medicine man began to paw among the objects he had spit out on the ground. Both the grasshopper and lizard were dead; and suddenly he pointed to the lizard. One leg had been severed from its body.

This seemed to call for a more serious plan of attack. The medicine man obtained a small bivalve shell from his assistant, and using the shell—a river mussel—as a pair of tweezers, he plucked a live coal from a nearby fire. He handed this to Gabrio, and for an instant I thought he was going to make Gabrio eat the live coal. But he quickly made it plain that Gabrio was merely to place the shell, with the coal inside it, in his mouth. The medicine man meanwhile mixed some dry leaves into an ash-like powder, and sprinkled the crumbled substance over the coal. It gave off a hot, penetrating aroma, something like bay leaves; and he helped Gabrio hold this in his mouth so that the fumes curled around his teeth.

After a few minutes Gabrio's expression relaxed. The pain left his tooth in a matter of a few seconds, and he turned to me happily and announced:

"Lizard claw smoke out tooth!"

This simple explanation settled matters as far as Gabrio was concerned. His pain was gone. It was "smoked out."

As we prepared to continue our journey downriver, I asked Gabrio if he would permit me to examine his tooth. I wanted to see the extent or type of infection that seemed to have caused the trouble, and if possible relate it to the witch doctor's fantastic performance. Gabrio either did not understand my request, or pretended not to understand it. He merely shrugged and said in somewhat jumbled explanation:

"Dogeetah he find lizard. He make sick."

The notion that the lizard had taken over the "spirit" of sickness that had caused the pain in Gabrio's tooth was not unusual. I have witnessed many witch doctors performing rituals since then, and I know that in each case sickness or even death is never attributed to disease as we understand it, but to a "bad spirit." It is the task of the witch doctor to locate that spirit and destroy or at least neutralize it.

Before leaving the village I secured some of the powdered leaves which the witch doctor had used in the heated mussel shell. I intended to make an analysis of the leaves to see if they possessed some healing or anaesthetic property. They did not. They were a variety of the babassu plant, with the properties of rotenone, which is used in a powerful insecticide. Apparently the leaves contained nothing that would cure a toothache or ease pain.

In Iquitos I found my old friend, Dr. Pereiro Cato, and immediately asked him for some explanation of the "cure" of Gabrio's toothache. He grinned affably, and said with a half-amused smile:

"You think you have found something new in medicine, eh? But perhaps it is very old—much older, even, than the medicine we practice. Is that possible?"

I told him I did not know what was possible and what was not, after watching a man cure a toothache by sucking splinters and lizards out of the patient's cheek.

He laughed again, and his black eyes twinkled.

"What you have seen might be a discovery to men in our

profession who do not go out to see things, eh, doctor? But you, Harry—you go many places and see many strange things. Tell me, have you not seen things you do not understand?"

I agreed.

"But what I cannot understand," I told him, "is how a toothache can be cured without medicine or surgery."

I told him I had examined the leaves, and had them tested. This was the only substance used that could be medicine; yet it had no curative properties.

Pips Cato touched his head with his finger.

"Perhaps it is up here, Harry. Gabrio may well have imagined it—and the brujo may very well have relied upon imagination to do the job for him."

"In what way?" I asked. "The toothache or the cure?"

My friend shrugged.

"Perhaps both. But let's assume your friend had a toothache. He had to have some kind of ailment—otherwise he would have simply deserted you, if he wanted to stop at the village. And the toothache was evidently cured. So your problem is reduced to a very simple one. How did the witch doctor effect the cure? Did the spitting out of splinters and lizards have anything to do with it—or was it just mumbo jumbo?"

My friend paused and looked keenly at me; and then he said:

"Let me tell you one thing, Harry—if you proceed on the assumption it is all mumbo jumbo, you will be wrong. And if you accept the theory that the mumbo jumbo in any way brought about the result, I think you will also be wrong. I say this from experience."

"What is right?" I asked. "You seem to have barred everything."

He shook his head.

"The answer is somewhere between those two points. When you are back in this country again, I will tell you where to find a strange man who lives up in the Jívaro country. His name is Pamantauho, and I call him 'Pimento' for short. He is not only a very good native doctor, but he is articulate and intelligent. In fact, in another environment he would be regarded as an intellectual. He does not even seek power in his tribe—and that is mostly what a witch doctor wants. He is a strange, interesting fellow."

I wondered what sort of fellow this intellectual witch doctor might turn out to be. My acquaintance with Gabrio's "dogeetah" had not been intimate. I had watched him work; but he had said nothing to me—at least nothing that I could understand.

"Does he speak English?" I asked Pips, of his witch doctor friend.

Pips said he did. "I have spent some time with him—at different times. He has many interesting theories about medicine. It would do you no end of good, Harrry, to go and see him."

The notion of visiting a witch doctor for post graduate training had not occurred to me; and in my particular profession, it did not seem to me that the Jívaro brujo—"intellectual" though he might be—could offer much. But I had become curious about the "treatment" that cured Gabrio's toothache.

It seemed to me that there were two factors, or conditions, that were so simple and obvious that no observer could fail to give consideration to them. The first was Gabrio's belief that the witch doctor was in touch with the spirit world. Most, if not all, South American Indians, and perhaps all primitive people, live in two worlds, rather than one. It is the same world to them; but in our eyes they are different—the world of reality, which we see around us, and the world of spirit. In many ways, the world of spirit to the primitive mind is not only a duplication of the world of reality, but is even more real. It is peopled by spirits, who are the souls of those who have died, or perhaps disembodied spirits having no human house for residence; or even the spirits of the woods —the river, the animals of the forest, such as crocodiles, lizards, snakes and birds. Gabrio, being an Indian, possessed all these beliefs, faithfully and fervently.

The second factor, or condition, is what we may regard in the sophistication of civilized ideas as credulity, but it is actually *faith*. Gabrio believed in the powers of the witch doctor who treated his toothache as completely and simply as a child reared in the Catholic faith believes in the wisdom of his parish priest. He believed in the witch doctor's powers even before they were demonstrated.

It is not too difficult to understand the witch doctor's "magic" when we begin with these two basic assumptions. They are not new assumptions, of course. They exist in most of the faiths of mankind, old and new. When they are applied to the more civilized segments of humanity, they become elements of psychological and sociological health, and even wisdom. When this kind of faith exists only in the relations between a witch doctor and his patient—or victim— there is a tendency to dismiss it as childish ignorance and superstition.

In this case, of course, I had more to go on than a sophisticated theory. I had seen Gabrio's toothache cured. I had also tested such medicinal ingredients as might have brought about the cure, and found nothing of medicinal value in them.

I was forced to the view that something more than medicine had done the job; and since I was not prepared to accept willy-nilly the theory of magic—which the brujo, of course, exemplified—I was driven toward the theory that there must be some element of psychotherapy in the cure.

At this point, I would have liked to have postponed my trip back to Philadelphia in order to investigate Dr. Cato's intellectual witch doctor more fully. However, I had patients of my own to consider, and it was not until the end of World War II, nearly ten years later, that I got back to Brazil and western reaches of the Amazon basin once more.

2

In 1946, about nine years after my first trip into the western Amazon basin and the uplands of eastern Peru and Ecuador, I accompanied the Roncador-Xingú Expedition into virtually unexplored parts of the Amazon country. This exploration into the heart of the Brazilian Matto Grosso is one of the great epics of adventure, obscured by the fog of war which then dominated the attention of other parts of the world.

The purpose of the expedition was to find locations for airways across the heart of Brazil. João Alberto Lens de Barros, one of the leaders of the 1928 revolution which unseated the dictator of Brazil, Washington Luis, and placed General Getulio Vargas in power, was the originator and guiding genius of this vast jungle operation. It was intended to explore and map more than two million square miles of virtually trackless jungle, inhabited by primitive and savage Indians, snakes, wild animals and poisonous insects.

The expedition covered a period of three years, penetrating

more than a thousand miles into the great interior plateau
of Brazil, from which the muddy Amazon is born. This fan-
like spread of mighty rivers accumulates the largest store of
river water in the world, emptying its yellow flood into the
Atlantic in such volume that the discoloration of the ocean
water can be observed more than a hundred miles from
shore.

I accompanied the expedition on two different sections of
its operations, as historian and anthropologist. On the first
trip, I joined the party at its base point, Aragarcas, on the
left bank of the Araguaia River which is one of the great
tributaries flowing ultimately into the Amazon at its mouth.
Before our boats could be prepared, the rainy season of
August and September approached, and it became necessary
to wait until the following year. I took the occasion to head
back to Iquitos, where I hoped to find my friend Pips Cato.

I found him in Iquitos, jaunty, genial and cynical, as always. He was "between jobs," having served for several
months as a medical consultant to an embryo rubber company; and he had accumulated enough money to tide him
over for a while. I tried to persuade him to go upriver with
me to visit his "intellectual" witch doctor friend, Pamantauho.

Pips grinned amiably, gave a quick tug of his pointed
moustache, and said quite firmly: "No thanks. I am a doctor,
not an explorer. I am also a philosopher. It is evil enough
that men like myself must work to live; but working for
nothing is stupid."

"There will be no work," I said. "We will go upriver in
a steamboat and float back in a canoe."

His sharp eyes twinkled, and he regarded me with friendly
pity.

"You have a great capacity for sticking your nose into

things that are not your business, Harry. Some day your curiosity will be your undoing, and then I shall be sorry because I will not have the pleasure of talking to you on your periodic visits to this part of the world. However, I shall live with a comfortable conscience, knowing that it is against my advice and wishes that you do these things."

He agreed, however, to tell me how to find Pamantauho. The witch doctor was of the Pauté tribe, one of the many Jívaro tribes which lived north of the Upper Marañón. Existing maps of these parts of South America are useless, as I found in my preliminary work for the Roncador-Xingú Expedition. Towns like Zamora are actually hundreds of miles from their apparent location; and some of the places designated as towns are merely a single trading post surrounded by Indian huts.

Between these few geographical landmarks are hundreds of square miles of virtually unexplored country, and a traveller must remain on the large rivers if he expects to get anywhere, or even survive. Dr. Cato pointed out for me, on a roughly sketched map, the location of Borja, one of the old, established Spanish settlements in this region. Beyond that the Upper Marañón curved through the gorge of Pongo de Manseriche, and from this point a tributary of the Pauté River would take me into the area where the big Pauté village was located—and here I would find "Dr. Pamantauho."

I was able to get passage at Iquitos, again on a steamboat, this time going as far as Borja, and another boat took me up-river some distance beyond that point. Here the Upper Marañón moves in sweeping curves, turning southward and even eastward, as it roams through the deepening gorges of the lower Cordilleras. The banks are high and the land is hidden by a facade of giant puna trees which raise their immense white stalks against the green background of the jungle.

Another guide, less amiable than Gabrio, took me into the tributary indicated on Pips Cato's map—apparently part of the Pauté system, although I could not positively identify it until I reached the confluence with the Pauté. The river was much narrower than the Marañón, and sitting in the dugout, I felt constantly the presence of lurking evil in the forest.

The water itself was lethal, filled with tiny fish that burrow into human flesh, entering through any of the orifices of the human body, and extending sharp spike-like gills so that they cannot be withdrawn. They are carnivorous, like the piranha and other Caribes, and feed on the flesh of the animals they penetrate.

My guide was a Pauté tribesman who knew of Paman-tauho. We paddled past a few small villages, with their thatch-roofed huts mounted on stilts—a protection not only against animals, but also against river waters which rise from thirty to forty feet in a few hours. This area has been flooded many times in the memory of people living today, and on some occasions entire villages have been inundated so suddenly that only a few inhabitants escaped, the others floating to the surface or becoming snagged in trees, where their rotting bodies were exposed when the water receded.

A growing sense of the unknown—the eerie, half-fearful sensation of going further and further into a land that is dangerously evil—seemed to pervade the walled-in river as we moved slowly upstream. The rhythmic dip of the paddle, almost imperceptibly heard amid the screeching noises of the jungle—the hoarse blast of a macaw or the sudden shrill staccato piping of some wild bird I could not identify—kept a constant cacophony of sound that accented the deeper silence of the marshes that lay behind the river banks.

Now and then my guide would stop paddling, and I would find my own sense agonizingly alert for the sound of whatever had disturbed him. Then, with no explanation or indication of what had arrested his movements, he would resume paddling, steadily and with no expression on his round, flat-featured face.

We came to a rounding bend in the river, and on the far shore—to our left—there was a settlement of perhaps thirty or forty houses visible from midstream. My guide grunted and headed toward this village.

The houses were built on a high bank, and only a few were on stilts, the rest being flush with the ground. Facing the river was an open clearing, and a large number of people —mostly women and children, since the men would remain indoors out of the heat during the day—were scattered around the central area. The huts were in the neat style of the Ecuadorean Indians, with thatches of straw for walls, laced in strips about eighteen inches wide. The roofs were compact and neatly trimmed. It looked like a good village.

We put our dugout in towards shore, where a number of canoes could be seen. The lack of curiosity about our arrival indicated that this village was not remote enough from the settlements to find anything strange in our visit.

A fairly tall, powerfully built man stood near the beach, apparently to receive us, or at least to find out who we were. He was naked except for a pair of short cloth trunks. He wore no shoes or sandals; and his only adornments were heavy arm bands, made of woven straw, and a purple head dress of beautiful flowing feathers.

I took him for the chief, and lifted my hand in greeting. He nodded.

"You are white doctor," he said. To my surprise he smiled.

I was startled at this greeting, because I had no idea that anyone—aside from my friends in Iquitos and the Indian guide—knew of my presence in this region.

I explained that I had come to see the "great Pamantauho" to learn from him the remarkable cures that made him famous everywhere. He grinned and nodded, as if he appreciated some secret humor in what I said. I wondered if perhaps I had overdone it. My purpose was to make friends with Pamantauho, and I had thought that if my admiration for his exploits were conveyed to him in advance, it would make my task less difficult.

To my surprise he said:

"Me Pamantauho."

He waved to one of the Indians who had come down to the water, and the man promptly seized the dugout and dragged it ashore. My guide helped unload the dugout, and the others showed great interest in the rather extensive camera equipment I had brought. They crowded around the dugout, chattering in a dialect that was not familiar to me.

Meanwhile Pamantauho—or "Pimento," as I later called him—guided me to a hut and indicated I was to make it my home. It was smaller than most in the village, and was near one of the largest huts, which I found out later was Pimento's home. Most of the houses were open under the eaves, protected against the rain but not against the winds. Pimento's large hut was a kind of temple, although not used for worship since most of the mass rituals of the tribe were held out of doors. A cluster of punha palms bent gracefully over the hut, which was perhaps thirty feet long and almost as wide. A square dirt platform was raised about sixteen inches from the ground inside, and Pimento sat on a chair on this dais.

He smiled in a slow, friendly way that seemed to hint at an inborn sense of humor. He spoke a few words of Portuguese and English, and with the aid of the smattering of local dialect I had picked up from my guide, we managed to communicate. The languages of these tribes differed markedly, and yet they were interrelated and mutually intelligible. I informed him of the purpose of my visit: to see for myself the wonderful cures for which he was famous even among the white people. He was extremely friendly, and did not even object to my taking pictures.

When I asked, "Do you know Doctor Cato?" he smiled again, in a friendly fashion.

"He know everyone," he said in Portuguese. It always seemed a bit strange, and yet somehow fitting and natural, that men like Pips Cato could travel these remote jungle trails, filled with lurking dangers and head-shrinking savages, as safely as they could walk the streets of a city. I presumed it was some message from Pips that had informed him of my impending visit.

Later, however, I asked him how he knew of my journey to meet him, apparently before I arrived. He grinned.

"The white doctor speaks through the air," he said, waving his hand at the sky. "So do the Indians."

When I told Pimento I was anxious to learn about the wonders of healing, it was neither politeness nor a desire to exaggerate that motivated my remark. I had heard stories of healing performed by the native brujos of this upper Amazon country that defied belief. Two examples of surgery will suffice: trepanning the human skull and the Caesarian section. Both are reputed to have been performed by Ecuado-

rean Indians and yet until only a few years ago they were
dreaded by surgeons of the Western world.

It was not long before I had an opportunity to witness
some of these marvels of primitive medicine—although I did
not see either the surgical operation on the human head, nor
the equivalent of a Caesarian section while I was in the Pauté
village. However, Pimento asked me to come into his hut
the day after I arrived, and I gathered from his wave of wel-
come that he was about to show me something of significance.

An Indian lay on a mat, his face painted with white and
yellow streaks and contorted into a mask of pain. One arm
was twisting spasmodically and awkwardly, and when I stood
over him to get a better look, I realized the arm was almost
torn from the shoulder. The joint had been virtually separated, and the flesh was torn on one side.

"Tigre!" Pimento remarked, as he squatted beside the man
and began to study the position of the arm, carefully and
methodically. Finally, when he seemed to have satisfied himself of all the elements in the dislocation, he gave the man
a drink out of a small bowl. It was a greenish liquid, and
although the suffering man gagged, he swallowed the stuff.
Then Pimento drank from the same bowl.

A few Indians, apparently relatives of the injured man,
stood at one side. Pimento did not speak to any of these
directly, yet every move and act seemed designed in part with
an eye to its effect on them. The patient lay on the ground,
his head rolling from side to side. Pimento's hands moved
swiftly, almost too fast for the eye to follow; but I distinctly
saw him take a thin wooden splinter from a small sack and
slip it into his mouth. Then he leaned over and appeared
to suck on the inflamed shoulder. I think he must have held
the splinter with his teeth and driven it into the flesh. The
man on the ground quivered and then lay still.

Pimento pulled his mouth away and spat out several objects, including a broken piece of jaguar claw and the splinter. I had heard that these Indians use wooden needles to inject drugs into the veins of patients or victims, and perhaps this was what had been done in this case. All the while he continued to mumble short phrases in the plosive local dialect. I vaguely understood, from the few words I knew, that he was calling upon the spirit of the man to return to the body and take up residence once more.

After the performance, I observed that Pimento himself seemed to be in a state of shock, probably as a result of the stuff he had swallowed. This practice, I was told later, is not merely to assure the relatives of the patient who are looking on that the witch doctor is not poisoning his patient since he takes a dose of his own medicine, but it is also a means of inducing a state of trance in the witch doctor. I gathered from later conversations with Pimento that he is not entirely aware of all that is going on when he is practicing, due to this state of trance.

When I asked Pimento questions about the stuff contained in the potion he had swallowed and given to his patient, he deftly turned the questioning back in my direction.

"White man make medicine good for white man, not for Indian," he said. "Indian medicine same—good for Indian, not for white man."

I never was quite sure whether these diversionary tactics were intended to conceal information, or merely to cover up things Pimento did not know. As I got to know him better, I realized how crafty he was. Pimento was not an old man; he was probably in his middle thirties, but he had been practicing the witch doctor business since he was a boy. During one of our long multilingual conversations he told me about his choice of and training in his profession. He had been badly adjusted to village life, kicked around by his playmates, and apparently had had strange dreams and hallucinations in which he talked with spirits. An old brujo took him under his wing, and trained him in the practice of the *curandeiro* or witch doctor.

During this training period, Pimento told me, he was not allowed to eat meat or fish, and for long periods he was not allowed to sleep. His old brujo tutor would slap him to keep him awake, and would blow tobacco smoke into his mouth, and then drop a solution of soaked tobacco leaves into his nostrils.

When he finally sank into a stupor, the old witch doctor would revive him by slapping him, and then spit tobacco juice into his mouth. Pimento became so sick he vomited until he was exhausted; and as soon as he was well enough to sit up, the process was repeated.

I asked him the purpose of this rigorous discipline, which did not seem to have much relevance to the curative arts, and he shrugged as he usually did, and said:

"Do white doctors go to school, or are they born doctors?"

It was difficult to explain the difference between training that aims at inculcating knowledge, and an ordeal whose only purpose seemed to be to find out how much physical punishment the candidate could take; and yet as I listened to Pimento, I began to understand the underlying principle in this kind of training.

It is necessary, of course, to think as Pimento and his old witch doctor tutor thought: that is, to believe in the inner powers and spiritual qualities of the practitioner, and that the ordeal of training enhances these. There was something in this discipline akin to the training of Stoics; and once, when I pried into this point in my talks with Pimento, he eyed me shrewdly and said: "It is bad if a doctor cannot stand sickness. How can he make his people well, unless he knows how bad it is to be sick?"

In subsequent contacts with witch doctors in other parts of the world, I was to find similar ordeals of initiation—among the Bapende tribes in Africa, and aborigines of Australia and New Guinea. The witch doctor or medicine man of any primitive tribe is the priest, minister to the minds as well as healer of the bodies, of his people. He advises them, protects them, cares for them, and in some rare cases, when he deems it advisable, he may kill them. With such powers and responsibilities, he cannot be less than any of those who believe in him; and if these ordeals of initiation do nothing more than weed out the unfit, they are of value. But they do more—they train the novice in the strength of body and character his job will require.

For example, the "ordeal of fire" among certain primitive peoples of Africa is preceded by a period of restraint from sexual activities. The candidate for priesthood who is being tested steps into a circle of fire, which is built up until the flames are crackling higher than the man's head; and if he has abstained from sexual activities during the prescribed period, he emerges unscathed. If he is not "pure," he cannot survive the ordeal by fire. The statistics on those who have passed the test and those who have failed are not available; but, as may be supposed, those who fail to come out unscathed far outnumber the "pure." The ritual indicates the belief in the mind of these people that "purification" by sexual abstinence gives greater persuasive powers with the spirits—a belief that is not uncommon in some aspects of our own culture. However, this ritual requirement is often provided with a loophole. One of the interesting points noted by observers of this ritual is that candidates for priesthood—particularly women—frequently confess that they have been unchaste, and are permitted to substitute sacrifices for chastity, thus indicating the practical as well as the spiritual character of the ritual, in providing for a good supply of qualified native priests.

A singular aspect of pre-witch-doctor training is the hint of a borderline psychotic or pathological state in the initiate previous to his preparation for the witch doctor's profession. Among the people of the Watgo nation in Australia, for example, one of the prerequisites for the sorcerer is that the candidate must have seen the ghost of his mother. Once a boy has confessed to this experience, he is placed under the tutorship of a witch doctor. In many West African tribes this kind of requirement exists, and frequently it brings into the profession a collection of neurotics and borderline psychotics. It is thought that these abnormal psychological states are proof of the ability of the witch doctor to communicate with and even control the supernatural spirits who have jurisdiction, in the last analysis, over the people.

Pimento had an innate perception of the psychology of people—not only of his own people, but of others like myself with whom he came into contact. Pips was right in calling him an intellectual. In a more civilized social environment he would have been a teacher or parish priest, or perhaps a psychiatrist.

Oddly enough, his position in the village was almost that of a parasite since he did little of the actual economic work of men, such as hunting and fighting. His youthful awkwardness, which led to his induction into the profession of the witch doctor, had barred him from normal activities of young men. He was well built physically, and it occurred to me that perhaps it was some lack of mental and physical coordination, such as epilepsy, that had created his childhood lack of adjustment to the normal life pattern for others in his village.

The characteristics of abnormal physical and psychological states, such as fits, trances, catalepsy or hallucinations, all fitted into the actual practice. Pimento would usually get himself into the mood for performing his curative feats by drinking some evil-looking brew that he concocted from the plants. In some cases he used a gourd, into which he poured one of his concoctions and then dropped in some hot stones. He put his mouth to the other end and inhaled the fumes, until the normal pupillary reaction of his eyes showed no optical consciousness. In this state he went through the ritual like a man in a trance.

His repertoire of techniques and abilities was unbelievably varied. He used drugs, together with his psychological devices, with equal facility for curing sores, improving upon both male and female fertility, predicting rain, delivering babies—in which he played only a consulting role—and all manner of small practice in the village.

One day I asked Pimento to let me watch one of his performances in the general field of obstetrics. A witch doctor does not usually act as a midwife, but in cases of difficult delivery, he is frequently called into consultation and may even prepare certain "magic" potions. In this case, the delivery was obviously difficult. The mother, a squat, black-eyed creature who lay moaning in her hut when I arrived with Pimento, had been in labor for some time, which is unusual with Indians.

I had heard of certain strange rituals for child delivery among the Indians of Central America, in which a witch doctor is called in to perform a long ceremonial in cases where the spirit of the mother seems to have been called away. This was apparently a somewhat similiar case. The girl lay still, except for periodic spasms, and her face showed the effects of exhausting hours of labor. I felt her pulse, and it was extremely weak. In one of our delivery hospitals, she would have required an immediate transfusion.

Pimento squatted before her, and laid out several articles —a curiously shaped stick, a piece of snakeskin, some leaves which he took from a pouch, a rattle made of a small gourd. He began to chant certain phrases which I gathered were an explanation to the girl of the departure of one of her spirits. It did not seem to me that she was sufficiently conscious to hear what he was saying; but Pimento continued in a chanting monotone to describe the departure of the spirit, and the steps he was taking to bring it back.

He even told of his conversations with the spirit, and he said she must not fight against the return of the spirit or it would never come back. Whether it was due to the opiate of his monotonous chant, or hypnosis, I could not tell; but soon the girl became quiet, and her spasms of muscular contraction appeared to be more controlled and less like convulsions. I felt her wrist once or twice, and the pulse was stronger.

Pimento continued to tell her of the wandering of the spirit, and finally announced that at the proper moment he would take it under his own control and reintroduce it into her body, so it could supervise the arrival of the child. The expression on the girl's face softened almost to a look of peacefulness; and finally as I watched Pimento's features, I could see that he was observing every change of the girl's expression.

Finally he signalled one of the women who stood by to perform the services of a midwife. In a short time the delivery began. During the preceding period no one had touched the girl. Everything that had been accomplished was purely psychological; yet from my own brief observations and from the changes in her pulse, I had no doubt that the girl had been close to death when Pimento began his ministrations.

The girl was delivered of her baby; and when I later saw her and the baby, both appeared quite normal and healthy. I asked Pimento how he had revived her physical strength, merely by talking to her. He looked at me with his dark, friendly eyes, and said:

"Spirit of woman did this. I bring back spirit after it went away."

"But you spoke to her, not to the spirit," I said.

Pimento nodded.

"She must know why spirit goes and when it is coming back. She must greet spirit," he said. "Otherwise spirit cannot go into woman's body."

It was impossible for me to determine whether Pimento believed this, or merely wished the girl to believe it. I knew it would be necessary for me to win the witch doctor's confidence in order to understand this important point. If he was deliberately practicing deception, there was the possibility that some kind of hypnotic treatment had been used. On the other hand, if Pimento also believed what he told the girl, he was using a psychological device that was even better than psychiatry, as we know it. He was, in fact, living out the conditions of her physical recovery—transferring his physical strength to her in the form of a flow of psychological force.

I felt as if I had lifted, perhaps ever so little, the veil of obscurity which shadows the relations between human beings —the silver thread that ties one mind to another, and perhaps even ties the living to the dead.

It was on the subject of death, however, that Pimento

elaborated even more than upon his practices with the living. He had the face of a doctor, but the eyes of a priest. When he spoke of living things, such as healing sores with which many jungle inhabitants are afflicted, or increasing the procreative powers of his masculine followers, it was with a kind of wry humor, almost with a touch of sardonic amusement, as if he recognized some of the spuriousness of his profession. But when he spoke of the dead, his calm face seemed to light up and the expression of his eyes became intense. His face was more massive than the usual Indian's, with great strength around the jaws and cheeks; and his dark eyes held both wisdom and kindliness.

"The curandeiro," he told me, "must know everything. If death is an enemy, he must know death. If he is afraid of death, it will kill him."

There is a crude logic to this point of view. As I watched his practice, during the period of about three and a half weeks I stayed at the village, I began to understand Pip Cato's reason for sending me there. I had indeed found an "intellectual" witch doctor.

3

---◆◆◆---

PIMENTO OFTEN HELD AUDIENCES with his people, sitting
on the chair a few inches above his clientele, who gathered
in his large one-room hut, either as patients or as witnesses
of his powers. On one occasion, he had just exorcised a
demon from a girl who was unfertile, sucked the venom of
a tiny orange-colored snake that had bitten an Indian on the
leg, using a mouthful of tobacco juice for the operation, and
was preparing a lizard-skin amulet to protect the victim of
the snake-bite in the future (the skin contains a scent which
mitigates against fear on the part of the snake, and therefore
the presence of its wearer is not likely to disturb the snake).

While he worked, I saw Pimento suddenly look through
the door. I thought he must have seen a strange bird, but
later I realized he simply had glanced at the sky.

He laid down the amulet and turned to me, and said: "In
two days rain will come. My people must be warned."

He left off making the amulet against snake-bite, and took
up a bowl full of a dark, brackish liquid. Later I found out

it was an alkaloid. The juice of a vine, known botanically as
banisteria caapi, was extracted by mascerating the vine into
a pulp, mixed with saliva. In some cases tobacco was used
for the same purpose. The pot, containing this mixture, was
placed on the ground in front of the witch doctor. He began
to sway back and forth, in a rocking motion. Then he started
mumbling strange words, which I did not understand, but
which sounded like prayers or incantations.

He sipped on the pot from time to time until it was empty.
Then an attendant ran and filled the pot again. It was evident from the strained expressions on the faces of those
around Pimento that they were prepared for a prophecy.
They leaned forward, with scowling, rigid faces, listening
intently.

The substance Pimento drank apparently was so irritating
to the digestive mucosa that it caused immediate vomiting.
He threw up the stuff he had drunk, and then drank more.
After about five doses of the stuff, his face achieved an almost
greenish hue, and he rolled over on his side and lay on the
dirt, retching spasmodically and groaning.

Suddenly he sat up and screamed some words in his native
tongue. Those in the room stared at each other, while Pimento repeated his cry three times and then rolled over on
his stomach and began to snore.

That night the sky darkened and it began to rain. I
quickly realized that this was not an ordinary rain. I awakened, hearing the lash of water against the crackling palm
thatches of my hut, and I remembered some of the things I
had heard about the floods that rose overnight above the
rooftops of a village and swept the inhabitants to their death.

However, the rain stopped by morning, and then I observed the people of the village moving their effects out of

the huts and carrying them into the jungle, which rose steeply behind the shelf of land where the village lay.

Pimento explained to me that he had forewarned the village of the danger of floods, and he advised me to lose no time getting out of the place. He said I might leave in my dugout, and float downriver on the current, or proceed with the inhabitants of the village to safer ground.

Since I wanted to find out as much as possible about Pimento's practices, I followed the tribe about three quarters of a mile to a place perhaps a hundred feet above the level of the river. My dugout was my only worry, but Pimento assured me there would be no danger. It would be held in a small inlet with the other canoes of the village, and would rise with the water.

Within twenty-four hours the downpour started again and lasted for two days. The gorges that cut through the rising hills behind us sluiced the water in great cataracts down into the valley, and the jungle was alive with creeping and crawling creatures, slithering toward higher ground. Actually, the flood did not rise beyond the lower level of the old village, but I felt it was just as well to be on higher ground. As I looked over the dark green flats, now half immersed in a gigantic mire of sodden branches and floating debris and dead animals, I understood the terrors nature held for these people— and the vital position of the witch doctor who stood as their sentinel, guarding them from swift disaster.

"How did you know the rain was coming?" I asked Pimento. It did not seem to me that he would claim that swigging down that frightful concoction of *banisteria caapi* could have given him prescience in a matter of this sort.

He grinned in an unabashed way, and said:

"The birds know the rain is coming. I know it is coming. When I get sick, my people know it is coming."

"But did you have to get sick?" I asked. "Why couldn't you tell them?"

He shrugged.

"If I tell, they forget. If I get sick, they no forget."

This rather ambiguous logic apparently was his only reason for taking the drink of the powerful alkaloid before making the prophecy. I began to understand some of Pimento's devious ways of instilling faith in his clientele.

I asked him why he drank the alkaloids, when he must have known the effect they would have upon his digestive system. He looked at me with his shrewd, bloodshot eyes, and said:

"I must keep my people from dying too fast."

I became intensely curious about the drugs he used. He seemed to employ them with a complete disregard for any fine line of distinction between medicinal and psychological therapeutics. At times I wondered if he bothered to make this distinction at all. While I stayed in the village, I found plants with known medical properties—quinine, ipecac, and even some of the modern "miracle drugs." Cocaine, for example, used to be imported from Peru, where it was known among many of the Indian tribes.

The knowledge of these drugs and their curative or medicinal properties was not obtained from any jungle laboratory; it was apparently handed down by word of mouth from one witch doctor to the next. The secrets were jealously guarded, and with all his friendliness, Pimento would not tell me how he knew about them.

There was one plant, for example, that is called *renaquillo*, that grows in the form of a shrub, or small tree. Pips Cato had told me it was used extensively for healing fractures, but is taken internally. The Jívaro tribes apparently have used it for generations; yet Pimento would give me no specific information about it. The reason is quite obvious: in his practice, the spirits perform the wonders, and the drugs are merely incidented by-play. I doubt if Pimento actually believed in the curative powers of some of the drugs he used. They were employed as window dressing. In the pharmaceutical lore of the Indians of Ecuador and Peru there must be hundreds of such drugs—and whether their curative powers are medicinal or psychological may never be completely determined.

Pimento's new hut—built for him by the communal labor of the villagers, since it was not proper that he perform any manual effort of this sort—was almost a duplicate of the old one. I helped construct a small hut for myself, and during the weeks I remained in the village, I listened to Pimento and watched his daily practice.

Probably the most difficult thing to understand about the primitive man of medicine is the blithe way in which he uses magic for highly moral and useful purposes.

One of the strange mysteries of the witch doctor's practice —at least to me—has always been the curious intermingling of good and evil. Pimento told me there were two kinds of witch doctors: the *feiteceiro,* or bad witch doctor; and the *curandeiro,* whose practice is to protect people of his tribe from evil spirits, predict the weather and perform rituals which will bring good crops and fertility to women of the tribe.

He described the curandeiro as a man who "protects" the tribe from any troubles brought on by the evil practices of a feiteceiro of another tribe, or even of his own tribe. A curandeiro must avoid mistakes, or his reputation is short-lived; and therefore he becomes a master at a kind of "double-talk" in which he uses the arts of a showman and the keen insight of a psychologist. He is also an astrologer, a weather prophet, and an agricultural expert, advising when to plant and when to harvest. He handles domestic problems and cautions young girls against the perils of promiscuous love. In short, he is custodian of his people, morally, spiritually and physically, and practices only white magic in their interests.

The feiteceiros, on the other hand, are practitioners of "black" magic. They often create sickness in a victim who is healthy, sometimes by suggestion and sometimes by the secret use of poison. Pimento also told me the evil witch doctor transforms his earthly body to some kind of animal—a snake, a vulture, or a crocodile—and kills his enemy or victim by purely physical means. It was never quite clear to me how much of this was imagination or fakery, and how much Pimento really believed. He spoke of psychological devices which seemed quite understandable and reasonable in the same way he talked of outright witchcraft, with equal conviction and with no particular differentiation.

The distinction between "white" and "black" arts of witchcraft, of course, is not peculiar to South American Indians. It exists also in Africa, in Malaya and Australasia, and in Oceania, where I later witnessed many of these primitive practices.

But Pimento was distinctly a curandeiro—a "white" witch doctor—and I felt he would not be likely to defend the practices of the "black" arts.

"How much of this do *you* believe?" I asked him. His amiable grin changed to a kind of sad smile.

"If a man is cured of an evil spirit, do you ask whether you believe he is well?"

"Suppose you have cured a man of sickness," I persisted. "If you do not know how you cured him, you cannot do the same for another man. In our country we study each cure so that we can understand it and make it better."

Pimento continued to regard me just a bit sorrowfully. "A doctor has no need to study the things he knows," he said. "But if the white doctors study these cures, perhaps they know how to kill the spirits of those sicknesses which we do not understand. In that case, there will not be too many Indians who die from the strange spirits of the white man."

The only spirits the witch doctors of South America really fear are those brought into the country by white men—such as tuberculosis and syphilis. These are "spirits" for which they have no remedy.

Pimento explained to me what he regarded as the real difference between the "good" and "bad" witch doctors; and I went to my hut and wrote down carefully what he said:

"All life belongs to spirits. Each man has way to reach spirits, to beg for his life or to ask for life of another. He does it with his own things—piece of wood on which he has spit, or drop of blood, or a hair. Witch doctor shows him how to do it."

He may show where the evil has entered the body, and he may also extract it from the body, or he may even shoot evil into the body with an arrow. However the cause of the cure is in the patient, and the cause of evil in the victim. The witch doctor does not appear to assume any real responsibility for what happens. He merely gets things in motion.

"Curandeiro does not know whether it is good or bad to bring spirits. But he must do it if he is asked to."

This ethical viewpoint is interesting. The witch doctor has no moral responsibility—only a social responsibility. He lives by his works and cannot hold his job if he does not work cures. A witch doctor is above all things a master psychologist.

I was particularly interested in the physical aids used by Pimento in his practice. He had an extremely wide and useful knowledge of the properties of various herbs and barks of trees, such as *cinchona,* which contains quinine, and is used by the Indians for malaria. Some of the herbs used by witch doctors, however, apparently had no particular curative properties, as in the case of the babassu leaves used by the Huambiza witch doctor to cure Gabrio's toothache. I was surprised to find that Pimento frequently used a practice in childbirth that is coming into prominence again in our own medical world—that of requiring the husband to lie beside his mate during delivery. This is not supposed to be a practice of the Jívaros, yet he described it in detail and seemed to understand the psychological theory behind the practice.

There was also a certain formula used by Pimento that interested me greatly. When I watched him in actual practice, he did not seem to be the clear-eyed, calm, "country doctor" personality that he appeared to be when I talked with him. In each case, he went through some preliminary performance to develop the proper "mood" for his practice.

During the years that had elapsed since I witnessed the "cure" of Gabrio's toothache, I had seen several other practicing witch doctors; yet Pimento was the first I had observed "in chambers," as it were. I could observe his mannerisms, his "bedside manner" for certain patients, a fatherly interest in others, and the cunning showmanship he employed for the general practice.

The skillful use of what we would consider psychotherapeutic techniques in primitive medicine, has been commented on by Dr. Claude Levi-Strauss, a noted anthropologist at the *Ecole Pratique des Hautes Etudes* in Paris:

"Most of us regard psychoanalysis as a revolutionary discovery of the twentieth century, and place it on the same footing as genetics or the theory of relativity. Others, probably more conscious of its abuses than of the real lessons it has to teach us, still look on it as one of the absurdities of modern man.

"In both cases, we overlook the fact that psychoanalysis has simply rediscovered and expressed in new terms an approach to mental illness that probably dates back to the earliest days of mankind, and which so-called primitive practitioners have always used, often with a skill that amazes our foremost men of science."

Among the problems which confronted Pimento, in his stewardship of the health, morals and the psychological well-being of his Pauté tribesmen, was the constant, ever-present menace of death in the jungle—whether from the poisoned darts of fellow Jívaro head-hunters, or the venomous fangs of the *shushape* snake that makes a sound like a bird to decoy victims within range.

I asked Pimento to explain to me what is meant by "death." He fumbled for a moment with a feather amulet he wore around his wrist, and then he replied:

"It is not my word, Senhor Doctor. It is your word. Each man has a spirit, other spirits do not belong anyone. When his spirit go away, it leave man without life—or maybe other spirit come into his body. That is what you call death."

Death, to the primitive mind, is caused by a "spirit"—either one's own personal spirit, that wanders off and leaves the body; or some alien or unfriendly spirit that crowds its way into the body. This concept seemed to be basic in the minds of curandeiros such as Pimento, and it was part and parcel of their "cures." It was also, however, basic to the feiteceiros, and the evil they practiced.

According to Pimento, if a man lying in a hammock goes to sleep and does not wake up, it is merely that his spirit has wandered off and has not come back. In certain instances, by leaving delectable objects around him and covering his face and body with an alluring grease made from animal fats and pounded leaves, the spirit may be induced to come back. But if it has decided definitely to stay away, there is nothing that can be done.

Since I was anxious to determine what part faith, or absolute belief on the part of the patient in the curative practices of the curandeiro, played in these "cures," I asked Pimento to explain his duties as tribal witch doctor, and what happened when his "cure" failed.

He grinned, in his amiable way, and asked me a question.

"Do white people always get well?"

I shook my head. It was quite well known that they do not.

He shrugged.

"My job is to keep bad spirits away from my people," he said. "If they die too much, they will need another doctor. Is not that way with your people?"

I agreed that there were points of similarity. A doctor whose patients seldom are cured would not keep much of a practice. However, there was a subtle difference, and I was determined to get to the root of it. Pimento's success—or failure—seemed to hinge not so much upon any medication or cures he effected physically in the patient, but in a rapport which he established by which the patient seemed to cure himself. The case of the girl in childbirth was an example of what I was probing for—an illustration of the peculiar influence which Pimento was able to exert on the patient, as a result of which the patient herself was able to accomplish her own cure.

"If you bring back spirit of a sick man, he will not die—is that right?" I asked Pimento. He nodded.

"Then," I said, "you should be able to keep everyone alive forever—since you only have to keep the spirit in the body."

Pimento grinned, intrigued by my discussion of his skills. "Old trees will die," he said. "That is because spirit has left them. It is so with old men—he must die, because spirit cannot live in his body. But if a young man becomes sick, it is because an enemy has called away his spirit, or driven an arrow into him."

Pimento's belief in mystical "arrows" was one of the most interesting facets of his practice. He spoke so naturally and convincingly about these "arrows" that I was sure he believed in their existence. Yet they were not material.

He believed that a witch doctor could destroy a man or maim him by shooting one of these "arrows" into his chest or neck. Frequently another witch doctor would be called upon to extract the arrow, either sucking it out or removing it by some incantation. I questioned Pimento closely about these "arrows," because they seemed to be both symbolic and psychological; and if they created disorders in the physical organism of the victim, they might be regarded as truly "psychosomatic."

"How do you get the arrow out?" I asked Pimento.

He looked at me with that wise and yet simple expression that had become quite familiar to me; and he merely said:

"If something inside skin, you must suck it out."

This was the procedure I had witnessed in the case of Gabrio's toothache, when the witch doctor had "sucked out" the offending splinter, grasshopper, lizard and what-not. It was also used, in a measure, in Pimento's treatment of the man with the torn shoulder.

Pimento also explained the way the "arrows" worked upon the body of the victim. Each part of the body, he said, is the same as the entire body. In spirit form, it grows to be the entire body. Therefore, if an "arrow" has been touched by some part of the victim—his saliva, or a drop of his blood—it can work its evil upon the entire body of the victim. Often this particle will be obtained while the patient is sleeping, and when the "arrow" later penetrates his body, it will grow in spirit form until it can effect his entire body.

Pimento told me that some practitioners of "black" witch doctoring often secrete poison in their mouths when they are practicing their strange art, and in such cases they may shoot an "arrow" into a victim while pretending to extract one.

The "arrow" itself might consist of a splinter, or even a piece of the victim's hair, as a physical symbol; but its lethal effect, I was sure, was psychological. Pimento even explained the use of the alkaloid extract he used from the *banisteria caapi* plant. He said it was to "keep the arrows out of my stomach."

He believed that without this protection, witches who hated him because he forestalled their efforts to bewitch his clients might shoot their own "arrows" into his stomach and kill him. I often thought that the accumulated effect of the alkaloids on poor old Pimento's digestive tract must have been painful enough to be regarded as an "arrow," but he never seemed to look at it that way.

During the weeks I spent with Pimento I was able to watch many of his operations more intimately than I had ever hoped for; and in each case I tried to relate what took place in terms of both physical and psychological therapy. He often spent days in preparation for a particular performance; and I learned from him that a witch doctor must abstain from sexual activities, take no food and in some cases refrain from talking to anyone for a certain period prior to performing a difficult cure.

Pimento's practice was entirely devoted to protecting his people from sickness and danger. When one of the villagers

came to him with an account of his troubles—either real or
fancied—Pimento would spend hours meditating upon the
nature of the evil, until he had assured himself of the proper
procedure to destroy it. At these times I did not speak to
him; but later he would always talk freely about the "cure"
and explain just how the bad spirit had been routed.

On one occasion I watched Pimento "extract" an offending
"arrow" from a patient's cheek. He employed almost the
same procedure I had witnessed before in the Upper Marañón country, when Gabrio's toothache was cured. But in
Pimento's case, I had the advantage of having talked with
him about the process; and I knew how much was real and
how much was faked.

For example, when he spit out the splinters, small strands
of cotton, an ant and a grasshopper, I knew they were real;
but there was no possibility that they came from inside the
patient's body. Therefore the cure must have been entirely
psychological. Pimento was a sleight-of-hand artist, in addition to his other qualifications as a witch doctor; and I have
no doubt he palmed these insects and slipped them into his
mouth at intervals.

He would mutter certain native words in a rhythmic
cadence, between periods of sucking, and this undoubtedly
gave him the opportunity to pass the next offending "arrow"
into his mouth. Then he would attack the patient with re-
newed enthusiasm, sucking on his cheek and neck, and spitting out another object. At times the patient winced visibly
at the exuberance of Pimento's sucking; but in the end he
appeared satisfied that his "miseries" had disappeared.

It is not unusual for a witch doctor to create the malady
and then effect the cure. He may shoot his "arrows" for
practice, and then accept the assignment to remove them.
The tribal people, living in awe and fear of the witch doctor,

seldom complain at this procedure, which of course would be highly unethical in our own society. Pimento, however, used his powers only for good.

I found a close parallel between the shooting of the "arrow" and the death-dealing sting of a venomous snake. At times, Pimento seemed to behave like a snake, poised and ready to strike as he discharged his practice "arrows" at a sleeping victim. There was even a curious sense of humor involved in this type of performance. On one occasion I watched him approaching a sleeping man and carefully pluck a hair from his head. He then produced a sharp splinter, and pricked his victim, drawing a drop of blood. The man was in a stupor from drinking the native drink of fermented fruit juice and spittle; and he seemed unaware of what was being practiced upon his person.

Pimento put the hair and the splinter with the drop of blood into an earthen pot and mixed it with some other ingredients. When the man finally awakened, he was told what had happened.

He came to Pimento, beseeching him to lift the spell. The man had no idea what would happen to him, but he knew the power of the evil spirits that Pimento could invoke. Oddly enough, there was no reproach of Pimento for the thoroughly gratuitous assault upon his spiritual well-being. He merely wanted to be cured of whatever trouble Pimento might have caused.

Pimento said nothing, and the man returned to his hut and crouched there, his head bowed in his hands. He remained squatting in front of the hut for perhaps an hour, a picture of utter dejection. I was about to ask Pimento to relieve the fellow's mind, when the witch doctor rose and walked over to his victim.

He delivered what seemed to be a homily on the wisdom

of a man not drinking too much, so that he exposed himself to evil practice; Pimento then went on to explain that he had not introduced any dangerous spirits into the man's body, but had joined his hair and blood to give him greater strength to resist enemy spirits—including the evil spirit of intoxicating liquor!

4

I MET Choro about a year after my visit with "Dr. Pamantauho," and even today he remains as one of the most accomplished practitioners of the witch doctor's arts that I
have known—hypnotist, ventriloquist, sleight-of-hand magician, professional psychologist and village priest, all wrapped
up in one wrinkled old man.

He was known for many hundreds of miles around the
village where I first saw him, in the massive jungle country
that lies in the heart of the Amazon basin, at the head of the
Xingú River. This long and winding tributary of the Amazon branches off to the west of the Araguaia, reaching southward into the upper plateau of the Matto Grosso; and in its
area of drainage are some of the most remote and untouched
parts of Brazil.

The second part of the Roncador-Xingú Expedition had
gone deep into this region, and I made several side trips for
the purpose of getting pictures for my historical and anthropological records. It was on such a trip that I met Choro.

Before I tell of his strange and in some ways fearful practices, however, I must recapitulate some of my own personal conclusions based on what I had seen among the curandeiros and feitecerios of Brazil and the brujos of the Peruvian Andes.

Two things I previously mentioned seemed to be present in every instance of witch doctoring I had observed. Firstly, primitive man lives in a harmony of two worlds that are equally natural to him—the world of everyday reality, and the world of spirits who populate that everyday existence for him. Secondly, he has absolute faith in the powers of the witch doctor.

No matter how fantastic and devoid of meaning from a biological point of view the rituals and practices of the witch doctor might seem to our more sophisticated civilization, they are real and tangible to, and they *work* for the primitive patient. This seems to introduce the factor of psychology and psychotherapy into the essence of magic. If we translate these jungle antics into psychological terms, we have something not unlike modern theories of psychosomatics.

The two principle psychological mechanisms, for example, which are used in psychotherapy—suggestion and confession—are widely used by the witch doctor. The process of primitive "brain washing" is essentially the application of the psychological principles of suggestion and confession to a subject to induce a state of absolute responsiveness.

The witch doctor, in effect, steps into the dark and troubled world of primitive man's mind, beset by fears and anxieties; and by the use of "magic" in various forms, he reduces anxiety and establishes faith. Nothing could be more in accordance with the principles of psychoanalysis and psychotherapy. The witch doctor, using the crude mumbo-jumbo of his primitive profession, gets results in a few minutes that some of our more costly psychiatrists require months and even years to accomplish.

The witch doctor really has a somewhat easier time of it than his more sophisticated colleague, the psychiatrist. He does not have to waste many hours in establishing rapport with his patient, since the very nature of their mutual primitive society has already done this for him. A witch doctor ministers to his own community, and is acquainted with the life history of each individual in it by virtue of being a next door neighbor. Furthermore, the primitive patient has known practically since he was born that the local witch doctor was the person to go to with all problems. This is a marked improvement over the situation in our society where, despite our enlightened intellectual recognition of the need for and value of psychotherapy, there is still just a little bit of something akin to shame in having the need for this kind of treatment. Also, the very simplicity of primitive life gives the witch doctor an advantage over the psychiatrist.

He does not have to clear away the complex psychological rubbish—which is a product of our tension-ridden civilization —that his more advanced colleague, the psychiatrist, often encounters. But until we begin to understand the techniques of the witch doctor in somewhat the same terms as we understand psychoanalysis and psychotherapy, we miss much of the essential meaning of what he does in his role as a doctor.

Choro was a doctor in the accepted sense of the word. He ministered to the needs of the sick and troubled people of a tribe of Indians in the upper regions of the Amazon River. He was a thin, hungry-looking man, with black, twinkling eyes that were set like fine, dark jewels in an otherwise disfigured and almost inhuman face.

Choro gave me my first basic lessons in witchcraft. Pimento had introduced me to the profession; opened the portals, so to speak, and let me peek in. But Choro was more than a common practitioner. He was a hypnotist, a ventriloquist, an expert at every kind of legerdemain. I have even seen him make a body disappear before my own eyes, when I was watching with sharp-eyed anticipation of his trickery!

I was on a picture-making expedition in the almost inaccessible regions that slope upward from the mouth of the Amazon to the great Brazilian plateau, which has its highest and most barren points on the rim of the Matto Grosso—the "Green Hell" of Brazil. A few bony shoulders of land rise beyond this point, but around them lies the vast mattress of green that forms the immense jungles of Brazil—so old, and so encrusted with rotting layers of vegetation that have been steaming since the dawn of time, that no living memories of today can possibly penetrate into the origin of this place.

Choro lived in a village that was similar to other native villages, a small group of thatched huts near the bank of a river. I had expected to spend only a day or so in the village, but because of Choro I stayed longer and learned much.

When I first met him, he clapped his hand to his nose in a gesture that would have been mildly insulting, if I had not been so surprised. Later he made it quite clear to me why this was done. Among the Chavantes tribes, to which he belonged, it is the custom to pinch the nostrils when a white man approaches. This is done so that no unclean spirit will enter the body of the Indian through his nose when a white man is passing. The gesture has no resemblance to its counterpart among civilized people; it is not a mark of disrespect, but an expression of the fear of the white man's "spirits" for which the Indian has no defense.

The element of fear is basic in all witchcraft and Choro was an expert in utilizing it as a psychological technique. In one case, which I was able to follow intimately, he used all the devices of a showman, magician and psychologist to control the superstitious beliefs of his followers and achieve an ultimate result which I firmly believe would have been beyond the range of our own medical science and of the talents of our most modern medical practitioners.

In order to illustrate the possible superiority of Choro's techniques over the practices of our own medical men, let me digress for a moment to describe an incident which occurred in our own society—specifically, at Duke Hospital in Durham, North Carolina.

Some time ago a man, about thirty years of age, walked into Duke Hospital complaining of a stomach ailment. He said he was suffering from stomach pains brought on by a business partner whom he admitted having "tricked" in their business affairs. He was in a state of fear, bordering on panic; and when he was asked for his diagnosis of his trouble, he said:

"I been spelled!"

He had been advised that a "doctor" at Duke Hospital—evidently a psychiatrist—had the power to lift the "spell" by hypnotizing him. The doctor to whom he presented his problem suggested that he enter the hospital for observation. The man stubbornly shook his head. If the hospital doctor couldn't "take the spell off his mind," by hypnotizing him, then he planned to see a "conjure man" who might do something for him. Apparently the "conjure man" succeeded where medical science did not, because the man later reported that he had seen the local practitioner, and his stomach pains had disappeared.

Dr. Vernon Kinross-Wright, neuropathologist at Duke, used this incident as a case in point to illustrate that there is an area of mental disturbance that had been ignored by modern medical science; and he felt this was evidence of a laxness on the part of medical men in not paying greater attention to the psychological elements of "hexes" and "spells."

He suggested that the mental processes involved were probably the working of a "guilt complex" in the mind of the supposed victim of the "spell"; and he thought the case of the man who had "tricked" his business partner should have been approached from this possible aspect.

The case which my witch doctor friend, Choro, was called upon to handle had almost the same elements that were involved in the case of the man who had been "spelled," although I do not believe that a "guilt complex" was the mental disturbance involved. Cases similar to this are not rare; I have seen native practitioners handle them in many parts of the world. They are far more common in dark corners of the jungle than in white-walled hospitals or psychiatric clinics. In this instance, it was in the darkest corner of the Brazilian jungle, that great mattress of green that has lain over half a continent for thousands of years, blotting out its dark secrets from the view of the civilized world. Yet it possessed the same elements that were present in the case of the man who was "spelled" in North Carolina.

Choro's patient also had a stomach ache. He also believed an enemy had "cast a spell" on him. And he looked to the witch doctor to protect him from this menace of evil.

Choro told me about the man's sickness, and asked me if I wished to come to his hut while he spoke to the patient. I quickly accepted the invitation, and found myself in a corner of the darkened hut where the sick man lay.

There is one thing I had discovered about Choro—and for that matter, most witch doctors. They do not try to fight the white man's sickness: The witch doctor knows he cannot combat dengue or yellow fever, and so he does not attempt to cure these diseases. He knows his patient will die, and there is nothing in his kit of medical cures that can prevent it. So this kind of sickness he accepts philosophically.

But when the malady is within the purview of his rude "science," he tackles it with energy and enthusiasm, and not without wisdom. Frequently he cures sickness that might have baffled modern medicine; and he does it with techniques that are unknown to many of our foremost men of medicine.

Choro told me the sick man had been laid low by a sorcerer from another tribe. He did not name the man, and I doubt if he knew who the man was. An enemy of his patient had presumably retained the sorcerer to "shoot arrows" into the man's stomach.

Choro said that since I was known to be a doctor among my own people, perhaps I would like to attend the performance. I think the old scoundrel knew from the beginning exactly what the trouble was—and what the result would be; but he wanted to impress me with his talents.

My own diagnosis was that the sick man had drunk far too much *tepache*, the local native beverage. I mentioned this possibility to Choro, but he shook his head. "This man too sick," he said. "Perhaps he die."

With this frank appraisal, he threw a gourd of cold water in the man's face—a form of treatment for similar ailments that was not without its counterpart in our own society. Then he turned the man on his back and stuck his finger down the patient's throat. At this point, he was proceeding, somewhat roughly, according to accepted standards of medical practice.

The Indian vomited rather violently on the floor of the hut, and I thought this should have eased his trouble considerably although he obviously was still critically ill. But Choro wouldn't leave him alone. He produced a kind of

native rattle, made of a dry gourd, from his tattered vest-
ments, and began literally to bounce up and down on the
patient's chest, screaming in a loud voice that drowned out
the agonized yelps of the sick man.

This, as I was told later, was to drive away the spirits who
might have lingered around the sick man, hoping to cause
more trouble. All the while Choro kept questioning the man
about his pains—when he had first felt them, and where he was
at the time. It developed that he had felt the first stab of pain
in the morning, when he was working among the plants
grown by the villagers for food.

Choro spoke hastily to the man in their native dialect—
which I understood to some extent—and I gathered he was
asking for the names of his enemies. The sick man held up
his hand and weakly enumerated five suspects. Choro nodded. Then he sent word to these five men to appear at the
sick man's hut.

The five suspects appeared in a short time and crouched
around the hammock of woven vines where the sick man lay,
moaning and staring balefully at the assembly of his enemies.
Choro had an air of professional sureness. After the men
had been arranged in a semi-circle Choro pointed to the
stain of the victim's vomit, which was still on the ground.
It formed an irregular pattern, like a Rohrschach ink blot.
He traced the longest tentacle to one of the five.

The man looked fearfully at Choro and then at the sick
man. The latter raised himself from the hammock and
pointed his finger at the accused.

"He is the one!" he screamed in the tribal dialect. The
man who was accused sat transfixed, his wrinkled face stiff
with terror. Choro stood erect, and waved to two Indian
helpers. In his tribe, the medicine men not only performed
miracles of healing, but he acted as a kind of chief of police.

All members of the tribe were more fearful of Choro's displeasure than that of the chief, who was an inconsequential old man who held his position as a result of great deeds performed in his youth.

The Indian helpers jumped beside the accused man, holding his arms against his sides. Choro stood stiffly in front of the man, pointed at him and uttered a sharp tirade, which I gathered from the tone and the few words I understood was equivalent to a formal indictment. The man was so obviously terrified that he was speechless.

He finally started to protest, but the two Indians hustled him off toward an empty hut that was a kind of stockade for the village. Choro then took the trouble to explain to me the significance of what had transpired. The man stricken with stomach pains was quite definitely the victim of an enemy who was a sorcerer. There were many such people, devoted to evil, Choro said; and it was not possible to ferret them out unless a sorcerer of greater powers intervened. Choro let me draw the conclusion that he was such a man.

I asked Choro what would happen if the sick man died. He grimaced slightly, and with a flourish of his hand indicated the fate of the accused. He went on to explain, however, that if the sick man got well it would be the result of one of two things: Choro, having greater powers than the sorcerer, would prevail over the spirits of sickness; or it was also possible that it was a case of mistaken identity.

This was not the end of the story; but I was able to make some analysis even at this point. The sick man obviously had complete confidence in Choro, and the accused man seemed to have much the same feeling, in view of his evident terror. Choro already had analyzed the outcome of the case; yet no one had made any effort to determine the real cause of the Indian's sickness. It was simply attributed to sorcery; and yet I was sure the man was really ill. No actual medication of any kind was offered, and I had a feeling Choro knew from the beginning that medicine would be futile.

I watched the hut in which the sick man was placed, and even went to the door to observe him. I was concerned about the lack of any real medical attention; yet there was nothing I could do. About midnight he died. Immediately the villagers emerged from their huts and ran to the stockade where the man accused as a sorcerer was imprisoned. The stockade appeared to be empty.

Choro walked carefully around the entrance to the stockade, examining the ground. Then he went directly to the hut of the Indian who had vanished.

That hut also was empty. Choro began a solemn march around the empty hut, chanting and now and then flinging back his head and waving his arms in a queer, rhythmic gesture. After about three hours watching this, I returned to my own hut and went to sleep. In the morning Choro was still marching. He continued to walk around the apparently deserted hut all day and all night and the next day. A small amount of food was brought to him in bowls, and he ate as he walked. Late the second night Choro stopped walking and signalled to one of his helpers. The man brought a tray of food containing dried corn, some cooked rice and plantains.

This was placed in the doorway, and then Choro went toward his own hut. I remained watching the food, and suddenly I saw a brown face emerge from the doorway. The accused man had been in or near the hut all the time, and I was sure Choro knew it. In fact, Choro must have seen him return as he kept his vigil. But for some reason he preferred this strange method of disclosure to simply sending his helpers in and dragging the culprit from his hut.

The man began to eat voraciously. I looked toward
Choro's hut, and the medicine man was standing in his doorway, calmly watching the procedure. He made no move to
seize the fellow; and finally the latter squatted down and
then rolled over. His body was bent double and he seemed
to be seized with spasms. I wondered if Choro had poisoned
the food, and I determined to ask him.

Within a short time the Indian was dead, and then I asked
Choro about the food. He picked up some of the uneaten
bits and chewed them, his wrinkled face almost expressionless. I was convinced that he had not put poison in the food,
even though he obviously might have been eating selected
parts that he knew were not poisoned.

I think the Indian died simply because he knew he was
going to die.

This was by no means the end of the affair for Choro. A
man had been proven a sorcerer in the eyes of the villagers.
Therefore the village must be cleansed of his evil. Large
gourds of *tepache,* the powerful fermented juice which the
Indians drink, and which in an overdose had caused the illness of the patient, were brought to the center of the village,
and torches were lighted. A fire was built and piles of food
were placed around the fire.

The "cleansing" of the village soon developed into a feast,
in which everyone ate prodigiously and got drunk.

On higher ground above the village was a large stone slab,
which served as some kind of altar. Sticks were gathered
around the slab, evidently for a fire. Several young boys
brought a pig and several fowl which apparently were to be
burned in the fire as sacrifices. The men formed a circle
around the altar, and began to chant and stamp their feet
rhythmically. I later saw dances in Africa which were quite
similar to this; and I have often wondered if the rituals of

witchcraft, such as dancing, are not as universal as witchcraft itself.

Suddenly Choro, who had been standing outside the circle, jumped into the ring and began to scream some kind of chant. His voice grew louder and louder, and finally he seized a chicken, put the entire head in his mouth and bit it off, and spit out the head.

It was a horrible sight. Choro's mouth was dripping blood from the severed neck of the chicken, and he began to walk slowly around the stone slab. He seized a burning stick from one of the men in the circle and brandished this with one hand, holding the headless and bloody chicken with the other. Now and then he paused before one of the men, and mumbled something. The men he addressed seemed to recoil first in fear, and then remained fixed in an almost hypnotic state. I observed one man in particular, who was holding a spear. Choro spoke to him on each round.

Finally Choro threw the dead chicken on the stone slab, and with his firebrand lighted the wood around the stone. Then he reached into a basket, which had been placed near the altar, and to my utter amazement and horror, pulled out a girl, about eight or nine years old.

He put his hand on the small of her back, and lifted her, holding the limp body of the child with one arm above his head, and turning slowly he walked around the fire now burning at the altar. I could see the face of the girl. Her eyes were open, and she seemed to be in a trance.

Choro continued to turn with the girl, slowly at first, and then with increasing speed. Finally he stopped and remained rigid for an instant. Then, with a thrust of his arm, he heaved the girl bodily into the circle of men.

At that instant I saw the man standing with the spear, directly in front of Choro. The girl's body flashed out into the glow of the fire, and fell toward the man with the spear. A great shout went up from the assembled Indians, a wild sort of cry that I can only describe as a purely animal noise.

In the dim light I saw the girl, held for an instant in the arms of the man with the spear. Then her body disappeared and the man stepped forward, brandishing the bloody spear.

This was the climax of the ceremony. I went to my hut, utterly sickened by what I had seen; and I determined to leave the village in the morning.

In the morning I saw the first real evidence of Choro's mastery of the arts of the witch doctor. The little girl, whom I had last seen soaring through the air toward the sharpened point of a spear in what I thought was a ghastly sacrifice to barbaric superstition, was playing blissfully around the village, laughing and decidedly alive!

I went over to examine her. There was not a scratch on her body. I went over to Choro's hut, and he was smiling benignly with his wrinkled, emaciated mask of a face. His ancient eyes seemed to regard me with quiet humor.

"It is the same girl," I said. "And she is alive."

He nodded.

"The good spirits are powerful. They bring life—they do not take it away."

I tried to analyse what I had seen, both from a medical and psychological viewpoint. A man had been stricken with a stomach ailment. It might have been any one of a half dozen kinds of stomach ailment; I had been given no opportunity to examine the man. It could have been poisoning, or acute indigestion, or a clogged intestinal tract—or it could have been psychological.

The sick man had died, presumably from his ailment. Before his death, he had accused another man—and that man had died. There was no physical evidence of why he died;

he simply died. He had been proved to be a sorcerer in the eyes of his fellow tribesmen, and he may have died from a guilty conscience, for all I knew.

But the aftermath was equally significant. The village had been "purged" by what seemed to be a human sacrifice; yet the villagers themselves must have known the little girl had not died, since she could be seen at play the next day. In our own society, Choro would have been exposed as a fake and a mountebank; yet he grinned knowingly at me, and seemed entirely satisfied with the results.

What actually had happened was an accomplishment of social justice—a rare balance that left all sides satisfied. Everything had been accomplished by purely psychological techniques—aside from the death of the man with a stomach ache. Even his relatives must have been satisfied, since the culprit had been ferreted out and destroyed.

Choro had achieved a balance in social justice, satisfied all parties—and was even more securely entrenched, if possible, in his post as curandeiro of the village!

It might be well to digress at this point in order to sum up my own observations, based upon what I had witnessed: and perhaps to enlarge a bit on what I mean by the psychological factors in the witch doctor's practice.

Our medical science has its roots in ancient China, Egypt, and Greece. Even in these civilized ancient lands, medicine was mystical and religious, concerned primarily with the relations of the body and the soul.

Only in the last three hundred years—dating from William Harvey's discovery of the functions of the human heart and the circulatory system—have these mystical and philosophical elements begun to disappear from medicine, replaced by the probing curiosity of Western scientific materialism. Instead

of believing that the "spirits" entered the body through the
mouth and into the lungs, reposing in the heart and frequently causing disease—as the Greeks believed in the days of
Hippocrates and Erisistratus—medical science began to examine the body with a view to understanding the physical
causes and cures of disease.

Medical men knew that pain usually accompanied disease,
and therefore they assumed that the mental maladies that
were sometimes associated with physical sickness were directly
or indirectly brought on by the wasting effects of disease itself, together with pain and discouragement that usually
occurs with any serious illness. In recent years this concept
has changed to some extent, with the introduction of what is
known as "psychosomatic medicine."

One of the important conclusions which medical men
have drawn from recent observations is that an inability to
resolve an emotional conflict is more likely to occur in cases
where the emotion is not in response to some external cause,
but is purely mental and stirred from within. Fear is an
emotion which may be either external or internal. Fear is a
natural and acceptable emotional reaction to a dangerous
external situation; but when fear or anxiety are aroused without conscious or tangible reason, the result may be mysterious and upsetting.

When known realities are not available to solve the
problem of emotional conflict, or emotional disturbances
such as fear, the emotional disturbance with its psychological
accompaniments is likely to be suppressed or remain incom-
pletely resolved, with the result that the equilibrium of the
individual is seriously disturbed. These unbalanced states
may result in permanent tensions which in turn affect
organic functions of the body.

The witch doctor, in practically every community of natives I have lived in or visited, is a highly trained professional man. He belongs to an inner sanctum, to which his forebears or members of a particular cult belong, and only a few in each tribe or locality are admitted. The fact that almost all witch doctors appear to be trained in a routine which does not vary from society to society as much as one might suppose, leads one to assume that they all have a basic knowledge of human nature. These practitioners of an ancient art are skilled to a very high degree in some of the techniques of mass control of psychological attitudes that modern science is only now beginning to understand. Many of their devices, with more "technique" but less common sense, are part of the paraphernalia the "psychological warfare" operative is using today.

The witch doctor understands the deep-rooted fears in the minds of each of his native followers, and the suspicions that are a result of these fears. He has his "bag of tricks"—devices by which he stimulates and manipulates the fears and suspicions of his patients. When he is called upon to cure a sick man, he directs his efforts immediately toward locating the source of trouble—either corporeal or non-corporeal—sure that this is the pathway to the only kind of "cure" his patient will understand. He frequently uses herbs and potions, but what curative medicinal properties these have is often problematical, and in some cases non-existent.

He manipulates the exaggerated emotional disturbances, which he may have helped to induce, with the skilled hand of a veteran performer, who understands and controls the emotional reaction of an audience. He may "materialize" a spider, or a lizard, using sleight-of-hand; and he works on an audience without skeptics. He may use hypnosis, or autosuggestion. He employs fetishes to induce faith. He may even kill to produce terror.

All these devices are cleverly woven into the fabric of what he knows his patient, or his victim, believes. But behind the techniques and the psychological mastery, there is the underlying current of strange powers—the causing of actual physical changes without a sign of physical agency to effect these changes. An aching tooth may get well; or a hand wither before the eyes; or a woman's face, lean and sharp, may suddenly assume the feline expression of a jungle cat—with claws that can rend human flesh!

5

———— ⊶⊷ ————

Later in the summer of 1947 I rejoined the Roncador-Xingú Expedition at an outlying base camp, which was called *Jacaré*. A small landing field had been built, with a radio station; and from this point the several parties of the expedition were to plunge north and west into the trackless heart of the Amazon jungle.

There were scores of rivers, winding like snakes through the green mattress of the jungle. We reconnoitered these in small airplanes, but in order to reach the villages we spotted it was necessary to go upriver in small boats.

My first contact with the Indians in this region was with the few who had been recruited for work at the camp. About a hundred men were employed, and they came with their wives and children. As they had only recently come into contact for the first time with white people, it was possible to observe the relative unacculturated and primitive state of their customs.

I became particularly interested in the "cults" or form of

"worship of the dead" that appeared to be the basis of the religion of these people. They, like any other primitive peoples, believed that the dead ruled the living. Even the airplane in which we landed was believed by the natives working for the expedition to have come from the "land of the dead."

In order to get such information as I could obtain from these sources, I made it a practice to pick up a few words of their language and to talk with as many of them as was possible, despite the rigorous conditions of the camp which was preparing for a series of new thrusts into the jungle.

Some of the practices relating to the dead are among the most mysterious, the most horrifying, of all the rituals of primitive people. These practices are to be found everywhere—in South America, Africa, Australasia and Oceania. In our efforts to study them, we embark upon a dark sea of troubled waters, where we lack charts, sounding lines, or a key to the meaning of death as those people understand it.

The primitive seems to be in daily fear that the spirits of those who have died will mingle with the spirits of the living. He sees no real difference between his sleeping state, when he may be in communication with those spirits in his dreams, and his waking state.

One of the first things I found out about these Brazilian natives was their belief in the power of witch doctors to "pray people to death." This is an extremely widespread belief. I once heard a story, on fairly reliable authority in Honolulu, of an American anthropologist who was making some investigations of the early Polynesians—on Fanning or Palmyra Island. A young native helper became infatuated with a girl in the village where these investigations were taking place, and the girl's lover employed a *kahuna,* or witch doctor, to pray the boy to death.

The usual rituals were performed. Some part of the boy's

clothing, or a stick he had spit on, was obtained; and with these the *kahuna* went to work. The information was conveyed to the boy that he was being "prayed to death," and he became sick. He was examined, but there was no apparent cause of the sickness. He grew weaker and apparently was well on the way toward death when the ethnologist who employed him decided that a form of reverse psychosomatics was in order. His powers of suggestion proved to be doubly effective. He assured the boy that he was a more powerful *kahuna* than the one who was praying him to death, and this information was conveyed to the other parties. The boy recovered—and the *kahuna* died!

In the course of my casual investigations among the Indians who were employed at Jacaré, I quickly found that this relationship between the living and the dead in the minds of the natives was a very tangible thing. This seemed to me to bear out a vague theory I had acquired from my talks with Pimento, and perhaps partly from my recollections of my visits to the Cheyenne Reservation years before with Robert Lame Deer. This theory was simply this: that primitive man has a closer kinship with the elements of the world beyond our senses than the civilized mentality. There seems to be less deception in his relations with the spirits of the dead; he knows that he can propitiate them with certain rituals or gifts; he is in a better position to defend himself against them than he is against living enemies.

For this reason he has learned to accept the reality of death far more readily than we do, even though he lives constantly in fear of it. He regards death as not only inevitable, but even imminent; and he becomes familiar with it. If this seems like a paradox, perhaps it can be explained in our own concepts of knowledge: things we do not understand may disturb and even terrify us; but when we come into closer contact with these things, and feel that we know them, we may still fear them but it is a more intimate kind of fear, and there is a fatalistic acceptance of the consequences.

The region into which the Roncador-Xingú Expedition was pushing was a part of Brazil into which no white men were known to have penetrated until about seventy-five years ago. Geographically, it lies along the longest axis of Brazil— a line from northwest to southeast extending more than 3,000 miles from Beranquila on the Colombian Coast to Rio de Janeiro. The entire territory of Brazil lies east of the 75th meridian, and a line south from New York would scrape the western edge of the country. This means an airline from New York or Miami would find its most direct route to Rio across the heart of Brazil.

The country into which we were penetrating lies along that line, from Manãos, which is near the confluence of the great waters pouring down from the Marañón, the Solimoes and the Negros into the Amazon. For more than 2,000 miles the route of such an airline would pass over almost unexplored country, rimming the rocky plateau of the Matto Grosso and extending over unmarked jungles in the steaming headquarters of the Xingú and Araguaia Rivers.

Development of such an air route would require a chain of airports, with hard-surface runways, radio facilities, ammunition dumps, repair shops and accommodations for passengers, strung across the jungles. From Manãos to Goyaz, on the eastern slope of the Matto Grosso plateau, there is hardly a spot on the map that can be described as an inhabited place.

As far as is known, the German explorer, Karl von den Steinen, was the first white man to enter this remote part of Brazil. He reported in 1887 the existence of tribes of Indians who appeared to have had no previous contact with whites. If the Spanish or Portuguese found them, no record of it has been located. A few intrepid Portuguese, such as Vasconcelos, who disappeared in this jungle more than thirty years ago, had gone into the heart of the upper Xingú River country; but nothing has been heard from any of them.

Shortly after I rejoined the expedition, we prepared to move in groups from our base camp into the jungle. Prior to my arrival at Jacaré, some of the reconnoitering flights had run into hostile bands of Indians, who shot arrows at the tiny planes, a few penetrating the wings and light fuselage. Consequently each trip into the jungle was preceded by reconnaisance flights, to try to determine the attitude of the various tribes.

Most of the Indians I had talked with at the Jacaré base were Trumais Indians, who belonged to the Carib group. In the area south and west of our base camp there were many different linguistic groups, including the Caribs and the Tupi group, to which a number of tribes belonged, including the Camayuras.

I was particularly anxious to see the Camayuras, because my Indian interpreter, Narum, was from this tribe. Narum had proved a most valuable assistant in my own work, compiling the records of the expedition and such anthropological data as I could gather. He was a powerful man, much larger than the average of his people, which was about five and a half feet. He had been with the expedition since the first Indians were brought in to work on the airfield, and spoke a smattering of Portuguese.

Narum showed me a string of beads, fashioned of river clam shells, cut to about a half inch in diameter and strung together. It had taken him six months to make the beads, each painstakingly cut and polished. There were about a hundred in the string, and they constituted a kind of insurance policy. He had a plantation up in the headwaters of

the Batovi River, a tributary of the Xingú; and in order to
get there each summer before the rains came, he had to get
a canoe from the Camayuras, who lived on the Kuluene
River. He always left his beads with the chief in trade for a
canoe. When he brought the canoe back, his beads were returned. He explained that if he ever lost the beads, he would
be late reaching his plantation, and the floods would wash
out his manioc crops and ruin him.

During the first weeks of our exploratory trips, both by air
and motorboat, we had an opportunity to visit about a dozen
tribes. Orlando Vilas Boas, who was known as the "great
white doctor" to the Indians, knew a smattering of many of
the dialects. Each tribe had a language of its own, but peculiar to the group to which it belonged, such as the Caribs,
Tupis, Arawaks, and the Ge groups, which included the
warlike Suiyas. However, the languages were all somewhat
similar, and the Indians of various groups were able to con-
verse with one another and to trade between tribes and
groups.

The Suiyas were notorious for raiding other tribes and
stealing women—a practice which was frowned upon by the
men of the other tribes, but not by the women. I had an
opportunity to talk to some of the girls in a Suiya village we
visited, and found they had no objection to being stolen. It
showed the manhood of their captors, and gave the women
an opportunity to travel.

One of the astonishing physical features of the Ge group
was a lip ornament worn by the men. Like most of the natives of this region, they ran naked, except for a large wooden
disc they wore in their upper lips, giving them an appearance
quite similar to that of the Ubangis of West Africa.

One day when we were flying low over the jungle in one
of the Waco planes which the Vilas Boas brothers, Orlando

and Claudio, brought up to Jacaré, we saw a fairly large village set back a few miles from the Kuluene River. This was the general area of the Camayuras, from which Narum came; and since his stories indicated they had not had any previous contact with white men, I wanted very much to visit the place.

We returned to the base camp, and I spoke to Orlando Vilas Boas, who was the leader of the expedition. His brother, Leonardo Vilas Boas, was next in line and Claudio third in command. They decided to make this trip with me, and assigned Orlando and a photographer. João Melim, to form a party of about a dozen men and carriers, and start upriver.

We followed the Kuluene for several days. Along the banks of the river, winding through the dense jungle, we found some of the most exotic floral coloring I have ever seen. This wildly beautiful accumulation of flowers and small, colored plants was not visible from the air, due to the overhanging branches of immense trees; but from the river it was a constant parade of the most fantastic coloring.

As we moved slowly upstream, I saw an amazing number of colored birds, also including jet black parrots—the first I had ever seen. Our boat was about forty-five feet long, built of solid mahogany, with a shallow draft that would carry us up any of the tributary streams for quite a distance. We were able to cruise close to the banks and inspect the terrain, which was soft and marshy for some distance beyond the shore.

After we turned from the Kuluene into a small tributary that we had spotted in our flight over the area, a strange sense of expectancy seemed to pervade the crew aboard the boat. I asked Orlando Vilas Boas what was happening.

"We have been seen," he said. "Soon they will meet us."

Within a short time, we saw a group of naked Indians

standing on a narrow shelf of land extending into the outer bend of the stream. The Indians were armed with bows and arrows, but there was no indication of hostility.

Whether they knew of our arrival through some "jungle telegraph," such as is used in Africa and in the great "Rain Forest," I do not know; but they seemed to have known in advance not only of our coming but of the peacefulness of our visit.

One of the first questions asked—which Narum interpreted —was for the "great white doctor"—the white curandeiro. Narum quickly pointed to Orlando Vilas Boas, and then he told me in an aside that this was "his people." In fact, his wife was in the village where these Indians lived, about four miles from the river.

The reputation of Orlando Vilas Boas as a great medicine man seemed to be current throughout the jungle area. In this case, however, there was a more specific reason. In the village, to which we were taken, there was a boy who had been at our camp at Jacaré a short while before, and had broken his arm. He had returned to the village, telling of the great miracle performed by the white curandeiro, which accounted to some extent for the friendliness of the Indians.

We spent several days in the village, and found to our surprise that most of the people in the village had never seen a white man before. The Camayuras, a tribe of the Tupi group, had little formal political organization. The oldest man in the tribe was "chief," and he happened to be the only old man in the tribe. His name was Tomaku, and he alone of the people in the village—with the exception of Narum, of course, who only returned to the village twice a year—had seen white people before.

He remembered Captain Vasconcelos, who was lost in this area and whose disappearance had remained a mystery. They did not know what happened to him, but Tomaku remembered that he had passed through this area.

I immediately asked Narum to inquire whether there was a witch doctor in the village. He grinned, and pointed at the jungle.

"He run away," he told me in Portuguese. "White curandeiro make more smoke!"

Shortly after we arrived in the village the medicine man returned. He apparently had left when he thought a more powerful witch doctor was arriving. I found out from Narum that it was not uncommon among these people for a witch doctor to leave when he had failed to prophesy rain, or his rituals and incantations had failed to revive a sick man. There was no punishment meted out for such failures; he simply lost his reputation and left, usually for another village where his failures might not be known.

This fellow was not as old as Tomaku, but was much uglier. His facial expression was so rigid that I concluded he was suffering from some mental trouble, possibly epilepsy, which is often a prerequisite for the practice of witch doctoring among some primitive tribes.

Through Narum, I was able to find out a good deal about the native beliefs and some of the customs. The old medicine man was the sole arbiter of spiritual matters, and he seemed to be almost senile. I asked him if he could control the spirits of the dead, and Narum, translating his reply, said:

"No, senhor. It is the spirits that control him."

From what Narum and the medicine man told me, it seemed evident that the idea of death in relation to moral or ethical values does not exist for the Camayuras. The notion of death as a punishment for some wrong committed while living made no sense to them. They had no conception of death as anything but passing into the "land of the dead." They did not believe a man went to a better place when he died, or even a place that was worse than the life they were living. A man or woman simply died, and his spirit continued to live in the "land of the dead," which was a replica of the land of the living, as it is for many primitive tribes.

I tried the same tack on the subject of disease, or sickness; and Narum and the old medicine man were equally vague.

"Spirit make sick," the witch doctor said. That was as much as I got on the subject. However, I gathered from some things Narum said that the Camayuras, like other Indians, believe death by any cause other than accident or old age, is caused by a "spirit," either of someone who has died or a spirit that belongs to no body and is trying to take possession of one.

The idea of "good" and "bad" spirits was not unfamiliar to them; but it was difficult for me to understand what they regarded as "good" or "bad." It was evident that a "good spirit" would not attack a person; therefore if a man were "possessed," it must be by a "bad spirit."

It seemed to me the Camayuras were about as close to having the most primitive concept of death as any Indians I had met. The disposal of the body was an example of this. The body is simply buried, as intact as possible, so that the spirit of the dead man will be able to communicate with his relatives in the form of dreams.

The belief that there is life after death is as natural to them as their belief in life itself—apparently since any other conviction would leave a vacuum in their minds. The Camayura Indians also see no difference between the spirits of human beings and those of any creatures, be they snakes, birds, fish or other animals. They believe that the dead may return to the world of the living by "possessing" a body—a belief held among many primitive peoples throughout the world.

There is also a curious corollary of this belief. If a man who has died has been attacked in the spirit world by a stronger spirit, he may be forced to take the form of an individual still living; and in this case exorcism by a witch doctor is necessary to remove the control of the dead spirit.

The witch doctor of the village—through Narum's interpreting—explained any of these beliefs with a simple and natural logic that defies the pedantic criticism of our more civilized minds. He said the sky is not a place of the future —as we regard Heaven; but it is the place of the past, where all our dead relatives and friends are living. Since the beginning of time those who have died have gone there; and consequently it is peopled with the first Indians who lived on earth. If it is possible, they will come back to earth, either as a man or animal; but the spirits of those who cannot come back infest the night, tormenting those who can return, or who are alive.

Most of the education in this tribe was limited to a study of legends and folk-lore, so that the young people would grow up knowing what happened to their forebears. In these legends there was little distinction between man and animals, or between the living and the dead. Stories were recited by the older men of the tribe, and were accepted by the children with a belief that compares with the faith Western children have in the existence of Red Riding Hood.

Naturally enough, they carry this uniformity of belief into their actual customs. The defeat of an animal is as much a triumph as the defeat of an enemy; and animals which do not prey upon human beings or are not used by the Indians for food are regarded as their social equals.

There was a feast in progress when we first arrived in the

village, and most of the men were gaily painted with a red vegetable dye known as *urucum*. The painting was in symmetrical lines, covering their faces, the upper parts of their bodies and their legs. The women wore no paint and did not participate in the dancing.

Most of the men were young, in their early thirties; and their appearance of good health seemed to contrast oddly with the early death rate. I examined several of the men, and found no skin disease or rickets, and no infections or deformities in their teeth and jaws. The frequent outbreaks of malaria might account for the early mortality. This scourge of the Brazilian jungles could be fatal to those who are forced to remain in the village or cannot escape from the infected area to a new location. I learned that when malaria appears, the people simply abandon their villages and move to a new and distant location. The rigor of the masculine economic activity of hunting also probably claims many lives.

A few days after our arrival, I noticed a circular hut, built like a smokestack, with no windows or doors. I asked Narum if he would show me what was inside the hut, and he scowled. It was the first sign of displeasure I had observed, and I became curious.

"Enemy?" I asked.

He shook his head, evidently reluctant to talk. Finally I managed to persuade him to elaborate further. It was a "peace bird," he said. No one must touch it, and only the chief could provide food for it. After some persuasion, Narum opened a thatch panel, and I saw a giant eagle, one leg tethered to a ridge pole in the center of the hut, supporting a roof. Narum quickly pulled me away from the place, and explained in Portuguese that as long as the eagle was held by the tribe, its members would remain in good health and be

successful in battles with other tribes. Whether it was regarded as a spirit, or had been trapped in some way, I could
not learn. Narum was evidently reticent about the bird and its
origin. He had been quite friendly to me, and rather than
jar the pleasant balance of amiable relations I did not press
the point with him or with Tomaku or the medicine man.

The constant interrelationship between the living and the
dead—and between the earth and the sky—was an essential
part of their living and thinking habits. I had some difficulty
getting them to tell me the legends of their people at first,
but finally a Camayura girl named Luruce, who had somehow become attached to our group, told me certain of their
legends. I had pointed to our campfire, and by signs and
words asked her where it came from. This substantially was
her story, as told through the words of Narum:

Once upon a time there was an Indian named Canassa,
who went hunting for game. He walked through the forest
until he came to a place where three great rivers came together. The night was coming on and it was becoming cold,
and Canassa needed a fire to attract the fish. He saw a firefly, and caught it in his hand. For a time he kept the firefly
in his closed fist, until a parakeet flew up to him and told
him that the firefly was not real fire, but would disappear as
soon as he released it.

"Where can I get fire?" Canassa asked.

"Only from the deer," the parakeet replied.

Canassa said the deer would run so fast in the night he
could not follow it, but the parakeet said: "I will make the
deer stand still by talking with it. Then you can kill it, and
let it die on the ground. The other deer will come around
the dead deer, and when you see the largest deer, you must
grab its legs."

Canassa did as he was told; he killed one deer while the

parakeet was talking to it, and when the other deer approached they dipped their horns into the carcass of the dead deer. All but one came up with their horns dripping blood, and Canassa seized the deer whose horns were dry, and the rest fled. The terrified deer asked Canassa to spare his life, and Canassa said he would if the deer would show him how to make fire.

The deer struck his horn against a rock, and told Canassa: "If you do that with your arrow, you will have fire."

Canassa broke the arrow into two pieces, held one section between two stones and taking the piece with the sharp point in his hands, began to twirl it between his palms so that the point ground fine dust in the hole it made in the side of the arrow shaft. This soon became hot, and a small flame appeared.

Since that time, Luruce said, the Camayura Indians have made fire in this way.

The functions of the Camayura medicine man were similar to those of Pimento and Choro, except on a much simpler scale. The lack of an elaborate social structure in the tribe, and the absence of a concept of divine punishment, made his tasks simpler. If he failed to cure a sick man, he was not blamed for lack of power, but because some other sorcerer had brought sickness to the victim. When this happened too often, he was not consulted or asked to perform his rituals, and he usually left the tribe.

His rituals were basically similar to those of other witch doctors or feiteceiros I had seen. He spat on an object taken from a suspected sorcerer, in order to cast a spell on the man. When a sorcerer was ferreted out, he was usually chased from the village, but was never killed—since death was not regarded as a form of punishment.

The witch doctor's prestige at the Camayura village had

suffered a setback prior to our arrival, and during our stay
he again disappeared. Narum confided to me that he was
probably afraid of a contest of skills with the "great white
doctor," Orlando Vilas Boas, and had fled to avoid embar-
rassment.

There was one custom which seemed to be the closest to
a regulated system of worship. That was the dance festival,
the *tanga tanga,* which was used to purge the houses of spirits
of the dead. This dance was designed to rid the village of
"bad spirits," and also to protect the spirits of their own
dead so that they would have easy access to the Camayuras'
"land of the dead."

This dance functions in part as a psychological release,
similar in many ways to the "possession dance" of Africa—
although I did not hear from any of the natives that they
believed spirits possessed the dancers. The dancers are decorated from head to foot with strange designs painted on
their bodies. The men of this tribe are bigger than the
average for this region, some being close to six feet tall and
weighing around two hundred pounds. They dance without
clothes, naked from their heads to their ankles except for a
G-string, made of peeled palm leaves and bamboo. On their
heads they wear ornate headdresses, made of toucan feathers;
and fiber bandages are wrapped on their ankles and wrists.
A trailer of monkey hair is sometimes attached to their hair
in the back, giving it the appearance of a flowing mane.

Each dancer plays a flute, blowing shrill, staccato notes; and
they maintain a rhythmic half-running stride. Under the influence of the dance they perform some of the most remarkable feats of physical endurance I have ever encountered.
They continue this rhythmic stride, half-running and half-
jumping, throughout a full day, from sunrise to sunset; and
then with hardly a rest, they continue dancing through the

night, weaving in and out among the huts of the village. As they approach a hut, they make three steps forward, and three steps backward; then they run into the hut and out again.

I cannot remember seeing any of the dancers take food or water during the entire day, and throughout the night it seemed to me—as long as I watched the performance—that they had no nourishment. In the morning of the following day their wives joined them as they continued the exhausting cadence, without breaking stride. The women ran beside them, with one hand on the shoulder, maintaining the same half-walking, half-galloping stride.

One thing I discovered after the dance: the men who ran through the huts blowing their flutes apparently blew some substance into the air which "fumigated" the place. Thus, in addition to a psychological release for themselves, they also drove out whatever influences remained in the huts.

Shortly before we were to depart from the village, I was awakened one night by Narum and told that the sister of one of the headmen of the village, Mondoro, was attacked by spirits. I went to the house—a huge one-room place, in which all the relatives lived and slept—and found the girl suffering from a post-natal infection. She was about sixteen years old, and had just given birth to a daughter.

I knew we ran the risk of trouble if any medical help we gave the girl should backfire; but I asked Narum to persuade the chief that we should take the girl back to our base camp. The next day we left, with the girl in the boat. She was in extreme pain, but she showed no sign of suffering beyond an occasional grimace.

As we rode downriver, we saw the "jungle telegraph" working. This is accomplished by beating on hollow logs, the reverberations sounding for miles through the jungle. Evidently advance runners had been posted at intervals on our route to see that we were not molested; and as soon as we passed one point, we would see the smoke of a signal fire drifting up into the clear tropical sky as an indication that we had passed that point.

When we arrived in Jacaré, the girl was in such bad condition that we had to send her in a plane to a hospital in Aragarcas. Several weeks later, when I was in Rio awaiting a plane to take me home, I heard from one of the Vilas Boas brothers that the girl had recovered and been taken back to her village. At least on this occasion, a primitive tribe's first contact with white people had been a happy one.

6

THERE ARE NEARLY seven thousand miles between the Andes and the Gabun country of West Africa, almost on a line along the equator from 75 West to 15 East, and yet the only basic differences I was able to detect between the witch doctors of both places was a matter of motives. Those of the African sorcerer seemed more sinister and less benevolent. Even that difference, however, is not clearly defined.

The best example of this I ever knew was Lusungu, whom the Belgians at Leopoldville regarded as the most powerful witch doctor, or *ngombo,* in the Bapende country which stretches between the Gabun and the border of Angola. She was about twenty-five years old when I met her—a sleek young creature with wild, dark eyes, a small, oval face and the classic features found among certain tribes in the Gabun country and the Belgian Congo.

Down the West Coast of Africa from the Bight of Biafra to the plains of Angola live the tribes of the Bantu nations, and here in the darkest shadows of the Dark Continent are

Choro, the witch doctor, and his wife in their village on the Araguaia
River in the Matto Grosso of Brazil

Ritual Kris Dance in Bali, photographed by the author. Participants shown here have reached a state of hypnotic trance which culminates in self-mutilation

Initiation of Bapende virgins into the Kiwele Secret Society. Photographed from a blind by the author, who secreted himself four hours before the start of the ceremony

"Pimento," or Pamantauho, chief of the Jívaro head hunters of the
Marañón in the upper Amazon country

An extreme example
of ornamental
scarification in the
Belgian Congo

The "orchestra" in the midnight ceremonies of the initiation of the
Bapende boys into the tribe when they reach puberty

The headman of a village in the central highlands of New Guinea

Pat Putnam, a New Yorker who went to the Ituri Forest to fight disease among the Pygmies and contracted a fatal illness. This picture was taken shortly before his death

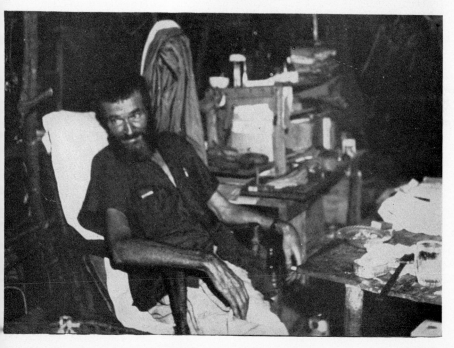

Witch doctors of Nepal exorcising evil spirits in order to cure a man of epilepsy

A "talking drum" of the Bapende. A small boy placed inside it answers questions the villagers put to the drum

Lusungu, a most extraordinarily talented female practitioner of the witch doctor's arts. She was both a Portia and a Lucrezia Borgia to her people, the Bapende of the Begian Congo

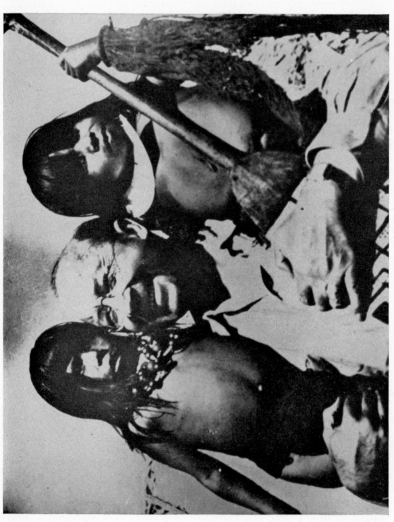

The author with Choro's children. Although their lives had been spent with their witch-doctor father, they quickly became friendly with the "white doctor"

found some of the most fearful practices of sorcery known anywhere in the world. Lusungu was an adept at most of these practices, although she was not particularly malignant, and at times even had a touch of material care for those who solicited her help and protection.

Women as practitioners of the black arts are no rarity in Africa. Among the Matabele tribes of South Africa, for example, there are actually more women practitioners than men. For reasons which Kipling made clear, they were more feared than the men.

Most witch doctors insist they practice only the "white" arts—the use of charms and fetishes and "casting of spells" for benevolent purposes, such as healing the afflicted, driving out spirits from the body, and predicting weather. They profess, at least to the white man, to deplore evil practices of witchcraft; yet even the most casual observer will find they employ the "black" arts, which are as much a tool of the witch doctor as of the witch. Such was Lusungu.

She was well known to most of the Belgian officials, but the name meant nothing to me when I first learned of her— even though I had heard of one incident in which she was involved. This concerned the strange killing of a Belgian police official in a rare and mysterious uprising of the natives of a Bapende village. The killing apparently was the result of the instructions of a "talking fetish"—an ornately carved figure called "Zinda," which seemed to possess the power of speech.

Many practitioners of sorcery use ventriloquism to enhance their mysterious performances, and a "talking fetish" undoubtedly would be manipulated by voice throwing. But it would be a powerful force for good or evil, since the tribesmen would follow its orders implicitly—and no Government official could directly assess the responsibility or punish the culprit!

The incident involving the "talking fetish" and the death of the police officer was often referred to as an example of the continuous problem of controlling the natives under the dark menace of fetishism; but I did not know at the time that "Zinda" was a fetish of Lusungu.

I arrived in Leopoldville, in the Belgian Congo, on a picture-taking trip that had led me through many of the countries south of the Gold Coast. The country varies in this area, shifting from the hot, parched plains of the North to the dense jungles of the Congo, and the flat country of Angola. On a suffocatingly hot afternoon I was sitting with a group of friends on the verandah of the Regina Hotel, overlooking the stream of people moving endlessly past us—that strange variegated assortment of faces, colors and costumes that is the mark of Africa.

This was a source of never-ending wonder to me; and I watched the faces moving by in white flowing Arab robes, the bright flashing colors of the East mingling with the smart tunics and white drill coats of the West. I listened indifferently to the hum of voices that always rises toward the end of the day, when the heat lifts slightly and people begin to sip cocktails and recover the use of their voices which had seemed to be suspended by the midday heat.

I noticed a little ivory mask that hung like a pendant from a woven cord around the neck of a peddler. This was the time of day when itinerant musicians and curio sellers walk among the tables in front of the Regina, where the hotel boys have set the accoutrements of drinking, and men meet to discuss affairs of the day, or just plain affairs.

The man who wore the ivory mask was of that blue-black hue that is found among many Negro peoples. His clothes and curiously Roman features stamped him as one of the tribesmen of the Bapende Valley. He wore a long white flowing robe, gathered at the waist in Arab fashion, and a high white muslin skull cap. He was taller than most of the curio sellers, which first attracted my attention; but the little ivory mask was the thing that really caught and held my eye.

My companion, a Belgian administrative official, noticed my interest, and asked the man in Kiswahili how much he wanted for the mask. The black man shook his head.

"He says he cannot sell it," my friend said. "It is a fetish of Lusungu, with great powers, and he cannot sell it."

"Who," I asked, "is this Lusungu?"

My friend explained that Lusungu was a woman witch doctor of the Bapende people, and that the curio seller would not only lose the powers of the fetish if he parted with it, but it might turn evil powers against him.

"Do you believe that?" I asked.

My friend laughed. "The curio seller believes it," he said. "Isn't that enough?"

The black man's face, smooth and crafty, suddenly became wrinkled with suspicion, and he glided off quickly among the tables. An Englishman, sitting nearby, leaned over and said: "I say, is that black fellow annoying you?"

I shook my head, and explained what I had wanted. When I mentioned the name, Lusungu, he became interested. His friend, Major Roelande of the Belgian Government Commission, knew the Bapende country, he said, and would know the female witch doctor. He indicated a tall man in uniform, sitting at his table.

Major Roelande was an affable man who had spent the greater part of thirty years policing the Bapende country. He was a seasoned, hard-bitten old soldier, with a ruddy face

and the polish of a veteran officer. He was typical of Belgian
Colonial administrators.

"So you want to meet Lusungu?" he asked, tweaking his
moustache in a gesture that told more than his twinkling eyes
and friendly smile. "She is worth knowing. But I don't
think she gives a damn about white men."

During the evening the Major told me a good deal about
the witch doctor practices among the Bapende. "We are
constantly having trouble with these fellows," he said. "All
the natives believe in what we call the 'black art.' They believe their witch doctors can ruin crops or bring rain, or
turn a man's best friend against him. They think these
fetishes can eat the soul out of people—literally eat the soul
while the body remains asleep."

He gave me a word picture of his impression of the witch
doctor: shrewd, overbearing, a master psychologist, with
secret knowledge and a mastery of tricks. They lived as
virtual parasites among the tribes, he said, doing no manual
or useful work, and exacting payment for their practices.
He also said they were not averse to drumming up business
in a manner that would be frowned upon as highly unethical
by white doctors.

"They scare their patients into coming to them for help,"
he said. "A lot of times we trace native trouble to things
they have cooked up—stories they themselves start to create
the need for their services."

Major Roelande told me of the strange case of the Belgian
police captain, Bailloit, who was killed by the Bapende and
cut into many pieces, each of which was given to a member
of the tribe who incorporated it into a fetish made by a
witch doctor.

"We sent out a detachment to find out what became of

Captain Bailloit. They found the poor fellow had been fed in small morsels to a crazy fetish they called 'Zinda'!"

He looked at me with his twinkling blue eyes, and added: "Zinda was the fetish of your Lusungu."

The phrase "your Lusungu" struck me with peculiar force. I wondered at the implication, since I had not met the lady and had expressed only casual interest. Yet I knew that I was quite interested; and I wondered vaguely if Lusungu could change the atmosphere with the effect of her personality so that even a wandering stranger like myself would feel traces of her spell even without knowing her.

At any rate, I knew I was interested; and when Major Roelande made a suggestion, I took it up with more than casual enthusiasm.

"You are near the Bapende country," he said. "Why don't you go down there and see her for yourself? I am sure it would prove interesting . . . I am flying over to Kikwit tomorrow, and I'll be glad to have you along. The Palm-Oil Company at Kikwit will lend you a truck when they go down to collect palm nuts, and I will furnish you with an official permit."

I was delighted with the idea. They all regarded me with a vague sort of amusement, but I was willing to take their jibes if I could have an opportunity of seeing this strange woman witch doctor.

The next day I flew to Kikwit with the Major. This town is in the lower part of the Bapende Valley; and here Major Roelande made arrangements for my use of a truck. There had been rumors of an outbreak of "red sickness" or measles in the area, and the superintendent of the Palm-Oil Company was glad to have someone with medical experience go to Kungu and Kilembe, villages where the company had palm-oil stations. Local representatives of the company who

had tried to immunize the natives had encountered trouble
with the *ngombos,* or witch doctors, of these villages.

We arrived at Kungu after a trip through low, sun-dried
hills, and were joined by a labor scout for the Palm-Oil Company, a fellow named Jerry who knew most of the local chiefs
and witch doctors. He took us to a native village known as
Musangalubany, the central village of a Bapende tribe led
by a wrinkled old pirate named Kalange.

When Kalange was advised that the purpose of our visit
was to immunize the people of his tribe, he seemed quite
friendly. He said he knew the power of "white man's magic,"
but he told us we would have to enlist the help of "the
great Lusungu," who lived about seventy-five miles further
into the heart of the Bapende country.

He agreed to send a messenger to announce our visit. To
fortify the messenger with sufficient credentials, a special
fetish had to be made. This was in the form of a wooden
mask, which Kalange himself invested with his own powers,
although he was not a practicing sorcerer. The chief told
us we would have to await the return of the messenger, which
would be in about two days; and then we might proceed to
Kinsambe, the village where Lusungu lived. This was not
far from the large native town of Kilembe, where the company's principal palm-nut holdings were located.

Jerry became an invaluable helper in this matter. He
spoke all the Kipende dialects fluently, and seemed to have
the confidence of everyone. I thought it was a far cry from
the days, not so long ago, when a labor scout was a precurser
of a hideous doom, who spied on the villages and advised
slave traffickers where they might recruit new supplies of
labor.

At Kilembe he introduced me to a Flemish gentleman
named Royale, who was the local Government commissioner.

M. Royale acted as an overlord or supreme judge, settling disputes where the Government was concerned, collecting taxes and directing the policing activities of a small but efficient native "army." He knew most of the sorcerers in the region; and in particular, he knew Lusungu.

Her village was about ten miles from Kilembe, and we went over in M. Royale's jeep. On the way over he chattered about the people and their strange native customs and practices, none of which he would disturb, except when the Government was involved, or there were some outrageous breaches of common morality, such as murder or human sacrifices.

We had driven perhaps four or five miles over the rough terrain, with little trace of a road to guide us, when M. Royale stopped the jeep suddenly and pointed excitedly at a group of natives, clustered beside the rough jeep trail that passed for a "road" in this locality.

We jumped out of the jeep and walked over to the group. The body of a young woman lay on the ground. M. Royale, as chief police officer for the region, ordered the body carried a little way off the road where he could examine it. None of the natives would touch the girl's body, however.

M. Royale looked significantly at me.

"You see," he said, lifting one eyebrow. "It is what we call murder by curse."

"You mean she has not been killed—she is just dead?" I asked.

He nodded. "It is not unusual," he said. I crouched down with him to examine the girl, where she lay in the road. In spite of the fact that the body had been lying in the broiling heat of the sun, it showed no signs of decomposition. I examined the eyes and then the head, and to my surprise observed that a piece of the skull had been excised. It was a small, elliptical piece of bone that had been cut out, and looking closer, I saw that the brains had been removed through this opening.

There was not another wound on her body—not even a bruise. I was becoming excited, because here appeared to be a definite case of the strange death practices about which I had heard. Meanwhile M. Royale was explaining: "The girl has been killed to appease someone," he said. "The witch doctor who did it had to bring back her brains—possibly for use as a fetish."

He spoke to the natives, who had gathered around us, plainly curious about the body, but keeping a respectable distance from it.

"This is Lusungu's work," M. Royale muttered. "She's the only one who could do it. At least, she is behind it."

I learned from M. Royale's questioning of the natives, that the girl was not known to any of them; or at least they denied knowledge of who she was or to what tribe she belonged. But they said there had been a strange absence of rain, and their crops were dying, and this in some mysterious way was linked to the girl's death. One said there had been sacrifices of chickens, and even a goat—a major sacrifice—but nothing happened. A "talking tree" had been consulted, and it seemed that this "talking tree"—a powerful fetish—had indicated that the brains of this young woman might appease the gods who had denied the area rain.

Later I was told that the girl had been friendly to a rival of Lusungu. This was a complication of jealousy and intrigue which seemed not unfamiliar even in our own society. The fact that the body had not decomposed was due to a native method of embalming. In a previous case, where a body was found without a mark on it, M. Royale had an autopsy performed and he said "the insides were bright red."

After jotting down a few notes, my host climbed back into the jeep and we headed for Kinsembe, Lusungu's village. Just before we reached the village, we saw a freshly dug trench a little way off the jeep road, near a clump of bamboo. M. Royale signalled to me to follow as he stopped the jeep and jumped out.

In the trench was the body of an old man, evidently the intended occupant of the grave. This seemed to be a combination of a murder investigation and "hounds-and-hares." I began to wonder how many corpses we would have to uncover before we found the culprit.

The preparations for burial were orderly. Across the foot of the grave were many articles, apparently the old man's belongings. There were rattles and feathered objects, and several gourds of palm oil. The burial apparently had been interrupted by our approach, or perhaps advance word had been flashed through the curious system of jungle telegraphing which many African natives use. This was not by the customary tom-tom, familiar to the readers of jungle stories. How word is passed I do not know, but I know it goes from village to village faster than a man can travel.

We went into the village, and M. Royale made his official inquiries. The old man was a witch doctor. He was known as *ngombo* or "Doctor" Witembe. M. Royale wrote in his notes: "Body of *ngombo* Witembe found murdered. Probably a feud among the witch doctors."

"He may have been killed in connection with the death of the girl," M. Royale told me. "Probably he had assured the natives that rain would fall if the girl's brains were brought in. When this was done and there was no rain old Witembe paid the penalty for failure. Anyway," he concluded with finality, "that's the case as far as the Government is concerned."

I was amazed.

"You mean you aren't going to investigate further?" I asked. "What about the girl—she was murdered, too, wasn't she?"

"The murder of *ngombo* Witembe explains the killing of the girl," he said, philosophically. "The killing of the girl explains the murder of Witembe. What else is there to look for?"

I was somewhat puzzled by this paradoxical concept of criminology, but I was soon absorbed in studying the large crowd of natives which had already assembled in the village to watch us curiously. The messenger from Kalange had announced our visit by leaving the mask, which had been made as into a fetish, hanging over the doorpost of the central hut.

As I walked toward the hut, I saw a native girl leaning against the doorpost of a new grass hut nearby. Most of the Bapende people were of blue-black color, similar to that of the curio vendor I had seen at Leopoldville, but this girl was of a light chocolate hue. She was taller than most of the other native women, slender and straight, with firm young breasts. She was naked to the waist and wore a loose-fitting skirt held around her hips with a sash. Her head was small but held erect with a kind of pride, and her eyes were slanted.

The most striking thing about her body—aside from its natural grace—was her stomach. It was covered with tattoo marks, which were composed of small welts forming a design in concentric circles. These strange marks were woven in the skin around her navel. I later discovered that the tattooing was done by making a small incision in the skin and introducing some vegetable dye.

Her hair was piled on top of her head in an inverted cone, which extended like a circular fan. It was held in place by some messy concoction of moss and animal fat. On the inverted base of the cone a row of brass upholstery tacks was impressed into the soggy mass of hair. The entire coiffure was so striking that the rather grotesque effect of the brass tacks was hardly noticed, and it became a flashing regal crown around her head.

She was watching us with half-drooped eyelids, like a sunburned version of Lauren Bacall. She even gave physical expression by a quick, swaying movement of the hips; and if I had not been so intensely interested in the scene that was developing before my eyes, I would have been greatly amused.

This was Lusungu.

She alternated between rolling her eyes and hips, and looking bored. Her face, carved like a perfect cameo against the black-green of the hut, settled into an expression of complete repose.

Under any other circumstances, the whole thing would have been overdone. It was like a burlesque, yet it was real. M. Royale was the first to speak.

"This," he said, extending his hand, and not even giving her the benefit of gender, "is Lusungu, whom you have come so far to find."

I felt slightly embarrassed at this forthright introduction, but Lusungu merely glanced at me with a slight flicker of interest, as if she had expected this all along. M. Royale walked toward her and spoke in the Kipende dialect.

He apparently told her who I was—a "white doctor" who had come to learn her methods of curing the sick. He explained that I had spent many months making this pilgrimage to her village. I was here to learn, not to criticize.

Her lips parted for the first time, revealing her teeth; and I must admit even I, who have peered professionally into

many mouths as a Philadelphia dentist, experienced a shock.
Among the Bapende naturally shaped teeth are regarded as
ugly. They are called "monkey teeth." Women undergo
long and painful ordeals of primitive dentistry in order to
have front teeth filed to sharp points, until they look like
fangs.

Lusungu's mouth was full of such teeth. She seldom
smiled, and when she opened her mouth and revealed this
ghastly row of distorted needle-like fangs, it was not a pretty
sight.

The sun had dropped over the edge of the trees behind the
village, and long shadows were forming in the open spaces
of the central clearing. It was a time of day when life begins
to settle down for the evening—whether it is in Rittenhouse
Square or a small village in the heart of Africa. Lusungu
lifted a hand gracefully, and seemed about to speak, when a
man ran into the village, his hands waving in wild gestures.

M. Royale quickly explained to me that he brought news
of a new outbreak of the plague in a nearby village. His two
daughters were sick, and he sought the help of the girl witch
doctor, Lusungu. He wanted to find out who was responsible
for visiting this sickness upon his family.

Lusungu stared quietly at her new client, and I did not
know whether she was going to ignore him or was trying to
hypnotise him. Then she turned quickly and gracefully and
disappeared into the hut.

After a few minutes she emerged, wearing coconut fiber
coverings on her naked breasts. A small boy came out of the
tent behind her carrying a marimba, a musical instrument
made of carved sticks fastened to a series of gourds. Lusungu
mounted a small platform beside her hut. The platform was
set upon four intricately carved figures, and I recalled the
ritual of "casting the sticks" in which four figures always

are used. It is practiced from one end of Africa to the other.

The distraught father squatted in front of the sorceress while Lusungu and the boy sat on the platform, the marimba between them. Lusungu began to talk in a low, half-musical chant. She held a rattle which she shook as she asked questions in a sing-song voice.

"Why did you come here? . . . Why do you consult me? Is it because you have no success with women—or is someone sick?"

The distraught father had already made the purpose of his visit clear to the girl, but she proceeded with these rhetorical questions and he sat in rapt attention. At intervals he replied to her, also in a sing-song voice. Meanwhile the boy shook the marimba, improvising tunes. The entire scene was strangely magnetic and hypnotic. I found myself following the cadence of the song and actually believing in all that transpired, even though I did not understand all they were saying and had to depend upon M. Royale to translate for me.

Finally Lusungu said: "It is the work of a fetish which you have in your house, or which has belonged to a *ngombo* who has left and now has come back. We must find out."

She suddenly tossed the rattle in the air, and it dropped near a white line drawn across the platform, parallel to a red line. This was the "casting of the sticks"—a witch doctor's ritual used in prophesying. A murmur went through the crowd of natives. The answer of the "sticks" was affirmative.

M. Royale leaned close to me and whispered, "She is going to make good use of the old *ngombo* we found by the road. She is a clever girl!"

Lusungu rambled on with her sing-song delivery, accusing the old *ngombo* of having brought evil to the family of her client—an accusation which was not likely to be repudiated, since the old man was dead. She said the evil spirit of the old *ngombo* had attacked the family of her client, because he had not come to Lusungu for help when his children had become ill.

The poor man was trembling, in a state of abject terror. He had stopped saying anything and stood watching the black sorceress. Finally she asked him for payment and he produced a belt of printed cloth. She dismissed him, advising him to go to the *ngombo y nyanza* of a neighboring village. He was a specialist on death, and might be able to save his children from the evil spirits which the family had foolishly introduced into their livers.

This was an example of monumental chicanery, yet it held the natives spellbound, in a kind of mass trance. I even found myself—with the aid of M. Royale's translations—following the performance with expectant and wholly credulous interest. Yet Lusungu had accomplished nothing!

After the terrified father left, presumably satisfied with Lusungu's practice, I began to analyse Lusungu's technique. She had actually accomplished only two things: she had frightened the man into believing that she had the power to protect him—if she wished; and she had also avoided the unpleasant possibility of failure. Her client had asked her the cause of the disease of his children and she had replied, apparently to his satisfaction. She had even collected her fee. Yet the entire responsibility had been passed on to the *ngombo y nyanza*, the specialist, in another village. This was not unlike some of the practices in our own society, in which a general practitioner may call in a specialist.

I took the trouble later to inquire into the outcome of the case, and was rather surprised to learn that the man had gone to the *ngombo y nyanza*, as directed. This functionary had made a mixture of palm oil and other ingredients which he sprayed over the body of the dead *ngombo*—after which the children recovered! Perhaps they would have recovered anyway. That is one of the intriguing mysteries which the occult practices of Africa always seem to leave behind, shrouded in a vague fog of credulousness and perplexity.

The day after our arrival in Lusungu's village another patient came to consult her. This time it was the father of a female child who had been raped. She was dying and needed medical aid.

We persuaded Lusungu to jump into our jeep, and M. Royale, the lady witch doctor and I drove over to the village where the girl lay dying.

She was about eight years old, and obviously had been criminally attacked. I felt her wrist, and there was no pulse. I took out my small kit bag and applied a stethoscope, trying to detect a heart beat. There was none.

"She is dead," I told M. Royale. But Lusungu, leaning forward over my shoulder, shook her head.

She crouched down beside the girl and began to breathe into her mouth. How she knew the girl still held the spark of life—when my modern medical instruments said otherwise—I will never know. But soon the girl's lips moved and I was able to detect a pulse.

Lusungu spoke softly into her ear, and the girl said, "M'buki."

That was the name of the boy who attacked her. Lusungu rose, and spoke to the natives who had followed us and clustered around the girl.

"Bring everyone named M'buki!" she commanded.

Five boys were brought before her. They were a forlorn looking lot, standing with their heads lowered. There was an abject despair in the attitude and expressions of all the boys that suddenly made me realize how completely Lusungu held them in her power. She interrogated each boy; and finally, when she received nothing but negative head shakes, she picked up the girl and carried her to the platform, which is part of the architectural accoutrements of every village.

Then she delivered the strangest homily on moral practices I have ever heard. None of the boys had actually attacked the girl, she said, although there was no question the girl had been raped. The evil *wanga* of one of the boys had done the deed; and this spirit was so strong it had not permitted the boy to confess. Therefore she would use means at her disposal to extract a confession.

The boys, ranging in age from nine to fourteen, stood with downcast eyes, yet with no sign of guilt in their faces. It was rather an expression of despair. Lusungu moved the boys toward the edge of the central clearing, and lined them up. Then she took a bowl which had been prepared for her, and passed this around to each of the boys. Without protest, each took a handful of the contents—a foul-smelling concoction made of manioc. They began to chew this starchy substance, until Lusungu said sharply in the Kipende dialect:

"Spit!"

The command was so sudden the boys did not have time to think about it. They spit out the partly chewed manioc and Lusungu examined it. Then she pointed to one boy and said: "You are guilty!"

The boy turned and dashed for the edge of the clearing. No one followed him.

"Let him run," Lusungu said. She pointed to the masticated morsel of manioc. "You see, it is dry. The *wanga* in the boy would not protect him, and he could not chew because his mouth was dry."

Later when we returned to Kinsambe, we found the runaway boy. He had run to the village of Lusungu, and had been held there until she should arrive. She looked sternly at the boy, and said:

"In three days you will die!"

She took a gourd of water from the river and sprinkled the water and pinches of some kind of red powder around the hut, where the boy stood cowering. He made no effort to resist her, or to escape. Later she spoke to the villagers, repeating her announcement, which was virtually a sentence. No one touched the boy. Three days later he was dead.

7

I**T MIGHT BE REGARDED** as a harsh judgment, bordering on injustice, to call Lusungu a murderess, even though there was no doubt she had contrived the death of three people. She had arranged for the killing of the old *ngombo,* Witembe; she had also arranged for the death of the girl; and in a sense, she had caused the death of a young rapist, M'buki. Yet it would have been difficult, if not impossible, for a prosecutor to have gotten a conviction in any fair court of law.

She certainly did not look the part of a wanton killer. She had raised the dead child in her arms with the tenderness of a mother.

I asked M. Royale, who had remained in the village to settle any disputes over the collection of the palm-nut crop, why the Belgian Government permitted her to remain free to practice her destructive arts.

He shrugged.

"She is really good for the people," he said. "They believe

in her powers, and if she was not here for them to believe in, perhaps they would follow someone less intelligent."

I gathered from his emphasis on the word "intelligent" that the Government found little difficulty in working out with Lusungu practical arrangements on matters which were of basic importance, such as the collection of the palm-nut crop. She had already acquired a plantation of her own as a result of the cumulative gifts of those whose benefactress she had been, and she seemed to be a responsible businesswoman.

I set about finding out some things about her, and strangely enough, this was not difficult. She herself furnished most of the information, through the interpretation of M. Royale. Her father had been a sorcerer, famed among the Bapende people for his ability to take the form of a leopard, an alligator or a lion. This was an exceptional gift among witch doctors. In some instances the witch doctor merely donned the skin of one of the animals and masqueraded in fearful dances, but in other cases the practitioner seemed to assume in human form the characteristics of the animal, even to bared teeth and slavering jaws, and often low growls.

It is legally a crime in most places in Africa for man to assume animal forms, and the penalty for killing such people is not too severe. A rival witch doctor apparently conceived the idea that if his men should kill as many of these animals as possible, one of the slain animals might turn out to be Lusungu's father. He ordered his followers to hunt down all the leopards, alligators and lions in the area and kill them.

While the penalty for killing a lycanthropic witch doctor was not severe, killing any of these three animals was a serious offense, and one of the hunters decided to kill the old *ngombo* while he was in human form, and thus spare himself a fine and possible retaliation from relatives of Lusungu's father.

He surprised the old sorcerer in the forest, and strangled him with his bare hands. Lusungu told me this story, simply and without much emotion. She looked at me from her drooping, slanted eyes, her small face calm and expressionless, as she spoke, with M. Royale interpreting the parts of her speech that I could not readily understand.

"It was easy to kill my father," she said. "He was an old man."

The man who killed him fled from the place, and by ill luck, he ran headlong into Lusungu. When I first saw her she was about twenty-five years old, and this had happened several years earlier. She probably had been a delectable-looking savage girl; at any rate, the man who had killed her father fell in love with her.

Lusungu had no particular affection for her father's murderer, but she wanted to be trained as a sorceress and she persuaded the young man to take her to the witch doctor who had been her father's rival. Her suitor paid out most of his earthly possessions for the training, and within a short time Lusungu learned so much about the profession that her lover suddenly and inexplicably died. This presumably was her first murder.

She spoke in Kiswahili, a basic language used by the Bapende and other people in the area, and M. Royale had to amplify certain parts of her story that I did not understand. However, I was able to watch her face closely as she talked, and it did not seem to me that any of these earlier adolescent horrors now caused the slightest emotional agitation.

She became a member of an organization that seemed to function roughly as a sort of "Witch Doctor's Protective Association." Her training seems to have been rather severe.

"I was told to do many things," she said. "Some were not good. I had to catch a big red land crab and take off the claws. I had to take the skin of a frog and the jaw of a monkey. These I pounded on a stone until it made a paste. Then I was cut here."

She pointed to her right temple. Small welts were raised on her skin, from her temple across her forehead to the opposite temple; and similar welts were raised in concentric circles on her belly. She indicated that the paste made from the crab claw, monkey jaw and other ingredients, was put under the skin and allowed to fester.

"After that they gave me medicine that made me feel sick for man," she said. This, I gathered, was some kind of aphrodisiac. Lusungu said she subsequently had used the drug frequently with clients who seemed to have lost the urge for love-making.

Later Lusungu was required to marry—since the witch doctors did not want to have an unmarried lady sorceress in their midst—but she did not produce the "husband" and I concluded he had gone the way of all flesh that crossed Lusungu's highly ambitious path.

While Lusungu talked, I gradually became aware of the strange, almost hypnotic effect of her eyes. She glanced coolly and unemotionally at me from time to time; and now and then I detected a trace of a smile, although her smile was little more than a widening of her full mouth, disclosing the sharp points of her teeth.

I asked her about the fetish known as "Zinda," which was reported to be controlled by her. She shook her head. This fetish, which Major Roelande had described in connection with the death of Captain Bailloit, apparently had belonged to her father. A white priest—as I learned from the Major, a Jesuit missionary named Father Delaere—had gone down to the village where it was kept and at the risk of his life had taken the fetish with him.

"Perhaps this allowed my father to be killed," Lusungu said. "It was a talking fetish and had great power."

Lusungu became so accomplished at the witch doctor's business, after her father's death, that she became "Keeper of the Fetishes"—a position of distinction even among witch doctors, since it meant that she had her own hut. Later, as her fees began to roll in, she acquired a small plantation and owned many chickens and even a few pigs.

She received payments for all manner of services, including weddings, and circumcisions and other ceremonies of adolescence for both boys and girls. Her fame as a prophet spread throughout the neighboring villages, and she was in demand as an oracle. Lusungu was also employed by secret cults to keep other witch doctors and witches from mingling with their members and casting evil influences upon them. She acted as a judge in disputes of ownership of pigs and even of women.

I sat in rapt fascination, listening through the medium of M. Royale's translation, to this weird story by a young Negro girl, who performed interchangeably the roles of Portia, Catherine of Russia, and Lucrezia Borgia.

She informed us that she did not prophesy the weather, because it was more or less fatal to many witch doctors, since they were held accountable if it did not rain after a positive prophecy. She told us of a witch doctor in a nearby village who had been called in by the families of victims of a strange disease. He agreed to fend off the evil spirits, but when a few more inhabitants died of the disease, he was accused of prophesying falsely and was brought before the chief. The *ngombo* asked for a trial by poison, and vomited the potion he was given to swallow, thus presumably purging himself. However, some of the more hot-headed villagers waylaid him and killed him, thus proving—at least in Lusungu's view

—that a witch doctor who loses his reputation will quickly lose his life.

I asked her what she thought of white men, but she displayed little interest. I think she talked with me because she knew I was a white doctor and she thought she might learn a few tricks from me. Most of her contacts with white men were with Arab traders, soldiers and missionaries, and she considered them all worthless.

She said she had never seen a white woman, but she had been told they walked beside their men.

"No man should let a woman walk beside him," she said. "His number one woman should walk ahead, so an enemy will strike her first, and the husband also can see what she is doing. Other wives must walk behind to carry things." She added that, in the native society of the Bapende country, only a prostitute walks beside a man.

I asked Lusungu what she thought about white men taking native girls as their wives. She looked at me from her slanting eyes, and her answer displayed rare wisdom.

"Take your wife from your own village. If you marry one from another village, she may be a witch and will poison you."

After we had been in the village several days, Lusungu informed M. Royale that she was going to another village where a local witch doctor had been ordered by the chief to find by divination a thief who had stolen some ornaments from the district commissioner's house. She had been called in as a professional consultant, and wanted to know if the white doctor would like to go along.

This seemed to be a good opportunity to observe the African witch doctor's professional procedures at first hand. We drove Lusungu over to the other village in the company jeep.

The local witch doctor was tall and powerfully built, with great scars across his chest, cut in ritually significant designs. His face was strong and angular, with thick lips which hung pendulously, and a narrow forehead, squeezed into a perpetual scowl. His face had been dusted with white ashes, and he slouched into the clearing where the "ferreting out" would take place, looking thoroughly disreputable and mean.

The witch doctor carried a leather sack and a gourd filled with water. He also produced an antelope horn, which was a kind of badge of office for a sorcerer; and with these accoutrements, he squatted on the ground and began to lay out amulets and a small collection of polished bones. He also poured some of the water in his hands, and sprinkled it around the ground in front of him. Then he shook a small amount of white powder from the horn, and seemed to be ready for business.

He lifted the bones, shook them and tossed them into the air. This ritual of tossing the bones, or its variant, the casting of sticks, was basic to most African divination proceedings.

The natives in the village had gathered around him with an artlessness that never ceased to puzzle me since they obviously exposed themselves to possible identification as the "guilty party." In this case the witch doctor drew a line from each bone—there were six—and pointed to the man at the end of the line.

The men were pushed out into the circle, and the witch doctor turned to the chief and said: "One of these men is the thief!"

The suspects were placed in a circle. The old chief was visibly angry, apparently because some of his relatives were among the suspects. He pulled a knife from a waistband he wore around his stomach, and brandished it over the heads of the men.

He chattered some words which I did not understand; and M. Royale explained to me that he was offering the guilty man an opportunity to confess and pay a fine. The men hung their heads in dejection, but no one spoke.

The chief became almost frantic in his anger. He shouted and gestured, and finally turned to the witch doctor and waved his hand commandingly.

"The thief will be caught, and he will die!" the old chief roared.

The witch doctor now came forward. I observed Lusungu standing behind him, and it struck me suddenly that she had now entered the case, advising him what to do. She took no part in the ceremony, but seemed to be watching the six men with fixed attention. Her black eyes glowed in the dark shadows of her face.

The witch doctor handed the nearest of the six suspects a small bird's egg. The shell was so fragile it seemed transparent, and it was obvious the slightest pressure would crush it. He directed each man to pass it to the next, and the one who was guilty would crush the egg and thus reveal his guilt. The natives crowded forward, more at ease now that suspicion was focused on the six men in the circle.

The fifth man took the egg, his face distorted with sudden fear, and a second later the tell-tale yolk oozed between his fingers. He held his hand out, letting the shattered egg shell fall to the ground. His eyes were white, and his loose lips began to tremble as he chattered suddenly what seemed to be a confession.

Then he straightened up and pointed to the dour-faced *ngombo*.

"That man and his brother, Kambula, help me steal!" he said.

Lusungu had slipped around behind the group, and was

standing close to us. She reached out and touched M. Royale
on the shoulder, and spoke rapidly to him in Kiswahili. He
turned to me:

"She says the old *ngombo* will be tried by poison—and he
will die."

I glanced at Lusungu, and observed a crafty expression on
her face. Suddenly it became clear what had happened.
Lusungu, by some subtle maneuvering—much of which was
lost to me—had contrived to put the old *ngombo* in a pre-
carious position. She undoubtedly had known of his complicity, and had deliberately permitted these events which
would disclose his guilt.

It struck me that she must be exceedingly adept, not only
as a practitioner but also as a politician, to be able to survive
professionally among fellow-witch doctors who must be aware
of her treachery. In the short time I had known her, she
had brought about the death of one colleague, whose death
entrenched her own power among the tribesmen; and she
had disposed of the girl, who apparently was a rival. And
now she had manipulated the practice of the other *ngombo,*
who had called her in professionally, to a point where he was
about to expose his own guilt. And in all probability, as she
had told M. Royale, the old *ngombo* would also die.

The accused man meanwhile was relating his own story to
the chief, now and then pointing a trembling finger accus-
ingly at the old *ngombo*. He explained that the witch doctor
and his brother had persuaded him to steal the ornaments
from the house of the commissioner, promising that they
would create fetishes that would protect him from Government charges. Now that they had failed to protect him, he
felt justified in accusing the old *ngombo;* and further he
charged the witch doctor, according to M. Royale, of having

permitted the spread of disease among the people of the village, resulting in the sickness of his daughters!

I suddenly recognized him as the man who had come to Lusungu for help, and whom she had berated for failure to come to her earlier. She had advised him to go to the *ngombo y nyanza* in the neighboring village—and this was the old witch doctor now under suspicion! By a series of Machiavellian moves, Lusungu was eliminating her professional competition.

Another *ngombo* was brought out to officiate at the trial which was to be an ordeal by poison. He was a thin, fierce-looking fellow with a human skeleton painted on his body; and he carried the inevitable antelope horn. He walked up to the witch doctor and pointed his finger at him, accusing him in a stream of chattering Bapende dialect of having brought sickness into the village.

When the accused *ngombo* denied having any part in bringing sickness to the village, the chief stepped in. This was a fine chance for him to make a show of it, and he did it in grand style. He ordered stools brought out for our party, and even assigned fan wavers to stand behind us and keep the air clear of insects. He was putting on a real performance for the white doctor—the ordeal by poison.

A large cauldron of water had been heated over a brush fire, and the bark of the *muhongoloka* tree was thrown in to make the concoction which would be used in the "trial."

Before the proceedings started, it was necessary for the second *ngombo* to complete his interrogation of his predecessor. It was somewhat superfluous, since the man had already been committed to "trial," but it helped create a sense of excitement and expectancy among the crowd of natives. The accused man did not even bother to answer. He simply stood in grim-visaged silence.

Some reddish powder was thrown into the pot to boil with the *muhongoloka* bark, making a thick, pasty soup; and while this was being stirred, a group of women moved into the circle chanting in monotonous cadence. Several drums began to echo in dull, rhythmic beats, and several bystanders started to jump about and to scream at each other.

The affair was working itself up to a feverish pitch, and the old chief seemed to enjoy it hugely, smiling broadly from time to time—in spite of the seriousness of the affair from a judicial viewpoint. The accused man stood a good chance of being dead within a few hours.

The second *ngombo* stalked over to the pot, peered at the gruelly mess, and then dipped out some with a ladle, poured it into another gourd, and watched it cool. He had an air of solemn importance in every movement.

The accused man was then asked to take a drink of the stuff. He did this, without any apparent nervousness, smacking his lips after the draught. Then the brother of the thief was given a drink, and finally the thief. All drank willingly.

The thief was the first to show evidence of sickness. He retched, and suddenly pitched forward to the ground and lay there, squirming slightly. The crowd dancing around them broke into frenzied shouts at this demonstration of "guilt." Drums boomed and the women chanted more loudly. Then the natives in the crowd began to move up and sip the poisonous brew, and in a short time they were vomiting all over the place.

Some of those who recovered jumped up and began to sing and shriek, and a few became so intoxicated they stumbled around and slashed themselves with knives. Blood dripped from their faces and bodies, but this merely served to increase their frenzy. The crowd soon became a swirling mass, and I turned to M. Royale, wondering if we might not be in some danger, but he shook his head reassuringly.

The commotion soon subsided, however, and when things were more or less quiet I asked Lusungu what the outcome would be. She looked at me in surprise, and said quietly:

"The evil *ngombo* and the thief will die. The thief's brother will live. He is not guilty. He will become the next *ngombo*."

We remained in the village until next day, and the following morning, true to Lusungu's prophecy, the witch doctor and the thief died. Their bodies were laid out in the village for the rites of burial.

The strangest part of this performance was the fact that the same concoction was drunk by half the people in the village, and only two died—the two predicted by Lusungu!

The only reasonable explanation I could think of was one that was not quite reasonable to my mind: The two died simply because they knew they were going to die. Later I asked Lusungu, and her explanation was even more simple:

"The lady witches in the village killed them. They did not like those two men."

I might have hazarded a guess as to who the "lady witches" she referred to might be; but there was nothing to be gained by raising this point with Lusungu.

Backtracking over the series of events to which I had been a more or less informal witness, I was struck by one thing: In no case was there any overt force, except perhaps in the use of drugs, if that can be considered a "force." The girl's brains had been removed, but this apparently occurred after death. The cause of old Witembe's death was problematical. There had been no sign of injury; yet M. Royale had referred to it as "murder." The young rapist M'buki had died without any evident use of force; he had been, in a sense, "persuaded" to die. The accused *ngombo* died presumably from poison—yet scores of others had drunk the poison and survived.

The only possible conclusion I could reach was that the lethal force of psychological suggestion was known to and used by these people. Undoubtedly there was also knowledge of some properties of the drugs used in the concoctions brewed by these witch doctors. The modern "miracle drug," serpasil, for example, was known to missionaries and medical men in Africa for years before it came into medical use in the treatment of high blood pressure and mental diseases; but for many years they had described its beneficial qualities in vain to Western pharmacologists. The *curare* juice extracted from the *sacha* palm was known to the *brujos* of the Peruvian Andes as a positive antibiotic for the cure of snakebite long before it was added to the pharmacopoeia of modern medicine.

Undoubtedly the witch doctors of Africa and South America knew a great deal about drugs and medicines that is not known to Western science, and the knowledge of these little-known drugs was a powerful tool in the hands of a witch doctor. But this cannot explain all of the things that puzzle us about primitive medical practices. It became evident, as I watched more and more of these fantastic events in a world that we usually regard as primitive and uncivilized, that they depended on the clever practice of applied psychology intermingled with a secret knowledge of pharmaceutical science. So adept are they that often our sophisticated sciences cannot comprehend their methods.

There was a strange story, for example, which I heard from fairly reliable sources, of an old *nyanga*, as witch doctors are called in the Tanganyika country, who was called into aid English officials investigating the death of a tribal chief. The old *nyanga* finally took the officials to the place where the body had been laid. In Africa, the grave site is usually selected because of its inaccessibility—to spirits, animals or human enemies. It was in the hot country south of Kilimanjaro, where the white hot sun blisters the land and where a body will decompose in a matter of hours. Since the purpose of burial is to protect the spirit in the body from molestation by enemies, human or otherwise, the body is not laid out flat in a grave, but is rolled into a compact ball and stuffed into the crevice or nook which is selected as the grave.

In this case, however, the body was stretched out flat, and according to the report of the officials, it showed no sign either of wounds or decomposition. The *nyanga* was asked to bring the body up for further inspection by an English medical officer, but he protested loudly that touching the body would forever render it incapable of hunting down the dead chief's enemies who had brought about his death.

"The chief is seeking the enemy who killed him," the *nyanga* said. "During this time his body must not be touched." Nothing would persuade him to permit the English doctor to see the body again.

A day or so later, however, word was received by the *nyanga* that the "enemy" of the chief had now been properly dealt with, and the English doctor might now examine the body of the dead chief at his convenience. They returned to the crypt, and this time when the blanket was unrolled, there was no body in it!

This startling circumstance immediately stirred the suspicions of the investigating officer, but he was assured by the old *nyanga* that if he made no report immediately, the body would be available that night for inspection. The story told by the *nyanga* was that the spirit of the dead chief had been engaged in tracking down those who caused his death, and his body must not be touched until this vendetta had been completed. The deceased had removed his own corporal remains to insure himself against such a violation.

The official agreed that he would wait until the body "returned." Nevertheless, he said, he must see it. Upon receiving his solemn word that there would be no physical contact with the body, either with the hands or with surgical instruments, until the dead chief had completed his posthumous mission, the *nyanga* indicated that he should look a second time. He flipped back the covering and the body was there—the skull caved in from a blow against the base!

Subsequently a post mortem was performed and it was evident the chief had been murdered. Whether the preliminary examination and the missing corpse were the result of hypnosis is a matter for conjecture. To the native, with his primitive conception of death and of the close communion between the living and the dead, this would be hardly a matter for speculation. But to the suspicious English medical officer, it must have been at least startling.

Scientific inquiries, even those concerned with psychic phenomena, have been unable adequately to explain this bridging of the gap between the quick and the dead. Yet primitive man spans it easily. The native sees nothing unusual in the clearing of this supernatural hurdle by his local practitioner.

In the case of Lusungu's victims, the transition from life to death may have been caused by perfectly natural means, which I was unable to discover. If so, the Belgian officials, such as M. Royale, also seemed unaware of such means. They apparently accepted the deaths as a phase of primitive cause and effect, natural only within the context of the native society. The methods generally were of little concern to them as long as the population remained peaceful. When something untoward occurred, however, such as the cutting up of Captain Bailloit, the gendarmes were sent out to look into the matter. But where only native victims were involved, the deaths were to be deplored, but otherwise disregarded.

Shortly after the "trial by poison," I prepared to leave the village of Lusungu. It actually seemed to me that she was sorry to see me go. Perhaps it was because I exchanged knowledge with her freely, and had displayed to her no preconceived ideas as to which practice was the better—hers or mine.

"You go back to your people, white doctor," she said to me just before I left. "You take something with you. You must also leave something."

"What should I leave?" I asked her.

"Rain," she said. "My people need rain." I recalled that weather forecasting was one part of the witch doctor's usual practice in which she did not indulge.

I laughed, and told her I had not brought the dry weather with me, and therefore I did not see how I could leave rain. She shook her head, a bit regretfully.

Some months later, when I was back in Philadelphia, I was somewhat startled to receive a letter from Mrs. Evangeline Mowbray, the wife of one of the Palm-Oil Company officials I had gotten to know well during my stay there. She wrote:

"Several days ago five Bapende warriors came over to the factory. They had been sent by Lusungu to inquire after you. Since you left her village, not a drop of rain has fallen. All their corn is drying up, and soon there will be nothing to eat.

"Lusungu thought that the *ngombo* with the four eyes (I wear spectacles) must have taken the rain with him when he left for his own village.

"Now, mind you, I do not think she is accusing you of theft. She merely would like to have you return the rain when you are through with it. I know this sounds silly, but it is serious to them . . ."

At first I thought this was some sort of joke, played by my friends in Africa. But after thinking it over, I sent a letter back to Mrs. Mowbray:

"I am glad you told me about Lusungu," I wrote. "I am very sorry to hear that all the corn is drying up. Will you please inform Lusungu that I am returning the rain, since Philadelphia now has more than it needs. Please thank her for the favor of letting me have it for a while."

This proves nothing in particular, but a month or so later I received this letter from Kikwit:

"Dear Dr. Wright: You won't believe this, but a few days after your letter arrived, it started to rain in the Bapende country. It has been raining ever since, and soon Lusungu will be calling on you to shut it off. Many thanks for your cooperation. Sincerely, (Mrs.) Evangeline Mowbray."

8

SHORTLY AFTERWARD I left the Bapende country, heading
north across Gabun to the town of Porto Novo, on the Gulf
of Guinea; and thence to Ouidah, the notorious center of
slave traffic in the days of the "blackbirders." I had a special
reason for visiting the "Slave Coast," and also a special invitation.

The reason was the reported revival of the fantastic "So-
Min Festival," or the "Annual Custom" as it was called in
slave-trading days. This an extraordinary dancing festival,
originally featuring the mass execution of hundreds of human sacrifices, who were beheaded in the market place of
Abomey, the capital of the Kingdom of Dahomey, as a tribute
to the ancestors of the king. Later sheep and oxen were sub-
stituted for human beings as sacrifices, but even in this modified version, it was as gory an exhibition as was to be found
anywhere in the world.

My special invitation was from Prince Aho of Dahomey,
the nominal ruler of the territory now known as the "Canton

d'Oumbegame." I had wired him for information about certain rituals reported still to exist in Dahomey, and he replied that I should come and see for myself. At that time I was making some investigations into African ritual worship, and so I set out in my jeep for the fabulous home of ancient slave-trading that gave the African "Slave Coast" its name.

Dahomey has three claims to fame: It was historically the wickedest and most notorious center of slave-trading in West Africa; it is also the home of the dread "Leopard Society," a secret cult of animal worshippers who are reputed to practice lycanthropy; and it was the original source of "voodoo" or *vodun,* a French version of a native word for ancestor worship and "worship of the dead."

There is probably no more spectacular country in Africa than Dahomey. The name itself is a European version of "Danh-ho-man," which means, "in Danh's belly." The story behind the name is quite interesting. Although Dahomey is now a French protectorate, known officially as the "Canton d'Oumbegame," it is ruled under French law by a lineal descendant of one of the ancient Kings of Dahomey—Prince Justin Aho Glèlè, who serves as the French high commissioner.

More than a hundred years ago Prince Aho's ancestor, King Glèlè, was the ruler of this little slave-raiding kingdom. He had inherited the title from an ambitious bandit named Dako, who was the first King of Dahomey.

Dako had lived in a small village near the site of the present city of Abomey, and had occupied himself with raiding neighboring tribes for slaves whom he sold to Arab traders. He kept widening his operations considerably, until he was poaching on the slave-raiding territory of a powerful neighbor, King Danh.

Danh finally became exasperated with Dako's operations

in his territory, and he brought a contingent of warriors with him to Dako's kraal, suggesting that Dako agree to stay on his side of the line dividing their tribal territories. It is reported that Danh angrily told Dako:

"You have been building around my feet; soon you will be building in my belly!"

Dako lost little time putting Danh's suggestion into action. He drove Danh out of his own kingdom, built a fine palace on the ruins of Danh's abode, and called his place "Danh-ho-man," from which the entire kingdom got the name of Dahomey.

Legend has it that Dahomey's founder, King Dako, was mortally wounded in battle, and called his eldest son to his side. He gave him his amulets, sword and scepter, and the admonition to "leave Dahomey bigger than you found it." So well was this injunction carried out that each successive ruler of Dahomey added to its wealth, largely through the sale of slaves, and it finally extended westward to the sea.

The nine kings who followed Dako increased the wealth and power of the little African kingdom until the French, who controlled most of the area, became alarmed toward the end of the nineteenth century, and deposed the tenth king, Behanzin. It was a satisfactory deposition for Behanzin, because he sold out for enough French francs to assure his ease and comfort for the rest of his life—and so the dynasty of King Dako came to an end.

The French established the Canton of Oumbegame with a "Chef de Canton" as ruler with modified power, and the descendants of Dako enjoyed that position under French protection. Prince Aho is a direct descendant of King Glèlè, one of the last of Dahomey's rulers and the greatest slave trader in West Africa.

There are grisly stories of the power and cruelty of the

kings of Dahomey. Under the pretext of "wars" to protect their boundaries, they would raid outlying tribes and bring back conquered tribesmen, selling the most able-bodied captives to the Arabs. The prisoners, now slaves, would be marched up to the port town of Ouidah, where they would be sold to English, Dutch and Portuguese traders, who maintained "corrals" or "kraals" for their human livestock.

The captured tribesmen who were not "marketable" would be herded into compounds at Abomey to await the "Annual Custom." Hundreds of these wretches were slaughtered in a public execution to appease with their blood the anger of the spirits that had caused such a poor lot to fall into the hands of the raiders. This ghastly spectacle took the form of a ceremony, with visiting notables invited to participate in the "sport" of slicing off the heads of the terrified captives.

The peak of the slave traffic came early in the nineteenth century, when the demand for slaves in the New World soared. King Glèlè, Prince Aho's great uncle, organized the slave raiding and trading so well that the Dahomey coast became known as the "Slave Coast" of Africa. The kingdom of Ashanti, the next largest and most powerful of the Negro nations on the West Coast, actually paid tribute to the Kings of Dahomey for the right to trade in slaves.

King Glèlè's success was due in no small measure to a man whose name is legendary in slave-trading circles—the incredible mulatto from Brazil, "Cha-cha" da Sousa. According to the best chronicles of the day, Cha-cha da Sousa jumped a Portuguese ship on the Dahomey coast and set up a slave brokerage business at Ouidah. He was black-skinned and a natural trader, and he quickly won the respect and favor of the tribal chieftains who dealt in slave trade. Among Africans he was a Negro, and among the white people he exhibited all the graceful mannerisms of a high-caste Brazilian.

He became a favorite of King Glèlè, and soon had an exclusive agency arrangement with the master slave-raider. He selected a beautiful hill in Ouidah to build a palace, near the ruins of the old Portuguese fort, which still stands as a monument to the lucrative business in which he was engaged. He also built a casino, furnished luxuriously; and his wine cellar, imported from Paris, was the envy of the Slave Coast. He populated the casino with beautiful women, many of whom were kidnaped. Whether they remained under duress, or simply liked the work and stayed on, they increased in numbers until Cha-cha da Sousa was hailed as the finest entertainer and the most lavish host on the Slave Coast.

Cha-cha da Sousa was reported to have displayed a sign over his casino bar which said in four languages: "Here you can surround yourself with all that can corrupt virtue, gratify passions, tempt greed, betray weakness, satisfy sensuality, but —you had better first pay for your slaves!"

When asked why he displayed the sign, Cha-cha replied: "Men who deal in slaves are themselves slaves to their weaknesses."

He made a bargain with King Glèlè under which he was given sole rights as slave broker for Dahomey as long as he lived; and when he died, he would leave all his wealth to the King. He died in 1849, leaving Glèlè his fabulous fortune, more than a hundred wives and mistresses, and approximately 150 children. It is said that even today in Ouidah, almost every other Negro answers to the name of da Sousa.

When I arrived at Ouidah, I found a car and chauffeur, sent by the Prince, waiting for me. The country between the coast and the city of Abomey rises in a series of rugged uplands, and the road winds through lush lands covered with well-tilled fields of corn and oil palms. For three centuries, under its bloodthirsty rulers and under the more benign protection of the French, it has been a productive and prosperous land. Behind the rim of coastal lands, however, are the dark jungles of the Niger Valley, for centuries known only to Arab slave traders and a few adventurous wanderers from the outside world—a land ridden with fetish-worship, the mysteries of ancient cults and the fearful practices of black witchcraft. Here the witch doctor flourishes as he does nowhere else in Africa.

From the moment we passed through the gates of the Prince's palace at Abomey, the air of ancient mystery which pervades the place was apparent. The massive brick buildings of the French colonial administration, standing at the opposite sides of the palace, were a background of security; but once we entered the palace grounds, this gave way to an atmosphere of barbaric but luxurious extravagance.

The car stopped first in front of a European house, where I was to remain during my visit. There were certain civilized facilities in the house, such as showerbaths and massive hand-carved beds. As I entered the house I saw wood carvings of leopards, a reminder that this was also the home of the secret "Leopard Society" whose rituals are reputed to be among the most devilish in Africa.

On my bedroom wall there was a carving, in bas relief on the hard mud surface, depicting a decapitated Negro with an immense knife held over him and his severed head lying at his feet. This gruesome reminder of the "Annual Custom" had a decidedly chilling effect on my spirits. It was certainly not scenery that would be conducive to peaceful sleep. Later I saw carvings of an almost identical design on nearly every

wall of the palace—an exhibition of barbaric humor, I suppose, permitting present-day guests to recollect with irony
the days when European visitors witnessed and even in-
dulged in the decapitation ceremonies.

Shortly after my arrival, a messenger arrived and took me
to the palace. We passed through a succession of chambers,
or courtyards, surrounded by hard mud walls twenty feet
high. The court of the Prince was not much different from
the great anterooms, except that the far side opened upon a
verandah. This was furnished with huge, carved tables,
chairs and statues. On a large divan, piled high with leopard
skins, sat a rotund, amiable looking man of swarthy complexion who was obviously my host, the Prince.

He was a strange-looking man. In his early days, I had
been told, he was slender and graceful, the suave "man about
town" of Paris, dark skinned and debonaire, with the manners of a courtier. He still had the manners, but he now
boasted a tremendous girth and an expansive grin. He was
about five and a half feet tall, and must have weighed 250
pounds. A high white skull cap was mounted on his head,
embroidered around the edge with gold thread; and he carried a scepter, intricately and ornamentally carved with minute drawings that apparently were heraldic insignia of his
family and symbolic of his rank.

He carried this over his shoulder, like a carelessly held
rifle. As I approached he jumped to his feet, almost rolled
off the divan, and came over to meet me, waddling along
with surprising speed and an air of cordiality that astonished
me. His personality seemed to sparkle from his sharp, dark
eyes.

Before we discussed the purpose of my visit, he waved to
one of his wives, whom I had noticed by the door when I entered. She crawled up to him, took one foot and kissed it,

and then repeated with the other foot. He spoke to her in
his native tongue, apparently ordering drinks. The girl said
something that sounded like "Yogh!" and left on her mission.

I learned later that Prince Aho had had only twenty wives
when he was made "Chef de Canton d'Oubegame" by the
French, but that he had since increased his household to sixty
wives.

Marriage, as a legal obligation, did not exist in Dahomey
when it was under the rule of its own kings. There were only
about 300 free souls in the kingdom, and all were members
of the royal family. Since all others were slaves of the king,
it followed that their wives belonged to the king. He could
confer the use of land or women upon any of his subjects,
and withdraw the favor at will.

There are several different ways of being married in
Dahomey under the rule of the French. A husband may pur-
chase his wife, with all her children; yet he has no legal
claim on the children resulting from his own or previous
marriages. They belong to the mother. However, he has no
obligation to pay his wife's personal expenses or taxes, and
she may keep her children as she wishes, regardless of his desires. Women are thus independent, and of quite high status.
In Aho's case, since it would complicate dynastic succession
to do otherwise, he retained possession of all his children—
although he did not have to pay for the upkeep of either the
wives or children. The French government took care of
that.

We had drinks of excellent French wine, and I explained
to the Prince why I had come to his "kingdom" in greater
detail than had been possible in my telegram.

"Your country is so fabulous, I feel it should be better
known," I said to him. He grinned, his black eyes twinkling
in his fat, friendly face.

"We are famous for many things," he said. "Today you see a modern city, with all the luxuries civilization can provide. But beneath the city there are still the bones of the past."

I could not help thinking, with an inward shudder, of the bas relief reminders of the "Annual Custom," I had noticed in my bedroom and on other walls of the palace.

"You will be interested in our dances also," he said. "There are many things in Dahomey that will be strange to you—and I shall see that you see some of them, and take your pictures."

The dance I most wanted to photograph was the famed "Leopard Dance," and I mentioned this. The Prince nodded.

"There are others, also," he said, politely. "There is the dance of thunder and the dance of rain. Our people have many powerful fetishes, which you may see, also."

I knew that Dahomey was one of the great places of fetish worship. The word itself is derived from the Portuguese "feitico," which means "to make." It refers to something artificially made, and believed to possess great power. The worship of these objects is found not only among the simpler societies, in point of cultural development, but also among the more complex.

The more valuable the objects used in the manufacture of a fetish, the more potent is the fetish. Therefore, anything pertaining to human beings is especially desirable for this purpose. Human eyeballs, particularly of white people, are highly regarded in the manufacture of fetishes, and graveyards are often broken into to obtain them. Parts of the heart and gall bladder, and human hairs, are important for use in fetish manufacture. These are variously believed to have power over, or the characteristics of, the entire body from which it was extracted, and can be used to cause disease, bad luck or death for the original owner, or to transfer his powers to the new owner.

In Dahomey, as in other somewhat sophisticated primitive societies, the economic needs of the witch doctor are provided for by others of the village, whether he is a full-time witch doctor or merely a part-time practitioner.

Prince Aho was an avid fetish-worshipper, and it was his close politico-religious relationships with the fetish priests of Dahomey that had actually resulted in his appointment as "Chef de Canton" by the French Government. He first tried to insinuate himself into the favor of the French when it appeared that the old Chef de Canton was dying, but certain elders of the old tribal hierarchy frowned on his pretensions and advised the French against appointing him.

Prince Aho went to the fetish priests, and a short time later the Chef de Canton died under peculiar circumstances, so that even the cause of his death was withheld by the authorities. It was reported in some circles that the "spirit of the leopard," a sacred symbol of the dynasty of King Dako, had invaded the palace in human guise and eaten the entrails of the old Chef while he was alive. Whatever happened to him internally, his exterior was badly marked by several deep gashes in his chest and the sides of his upper body. These gashes looked remarkably like the goring of a set of claws; and in his weakened condition he quickly succumbed.

The tribal elders consulted the fetish priests to determine a logical successor to be recommended to the French. These fetish priests, who had previously been consulted by Prince Aho, held rituals of communication with the fetishes of the dead Kings of Dahomey, and came up with the conclusion that Prince Aho was the logical successor.

The French, aware of Prince Aho's power with the fetish priests, and the consequent control he would have over the

natives, were satisfied with the recommendation, and ap-
pointed him as the new "Chef." He was invited to attend the
World's Fair in Paris in 1931 and remained there for three
years, during which time he became famed as an entertainer
and *bon vivant*. He met important officials of the French
Colonial administration, and when he returned to Dahomey
he put into effect several financial and administrative reforms
that placed Dahomey in a sound position economically, win-
ning the respect of the tribal elders and retaining, of course,
the close association with the fetish priests. It was really
quite clever of the French colonial policy to provide this in-
service training.

I had noticed certain queer markings on Prince Aho's face.
There were several parallel scars on each cheek, about a half-
inch long and obviously of ritual significance. I asked one of
the French administrative officers about these scars, and he
told me it was the "sign of Agassou," or the "Leopard Claw."
The scars either were tattoo marks designed to resemble the
tears of leopard's claws, or they were actually the marks of
claws. I asked the French official, but he did not know.

He told me a strange story. A leopard was believed to
have killed two children in a village near Abomey. The children showed unmistakable signs of the leopard's claws. The
tribesmen refused to join a hunt for the leopard, however,
the head witch doctor insisting that a witch, in the form of
a leopard, had attacked the children to bring discredit upon
the "Agassou." A detachment of French police was dispatched to track down the leopard, and they returned with
the carcass of the huge animal, which they staked out in the
middle of the village. The fetish priests, who had warned
the tribesmen against taking part in the hunt because it
would incur the wrath of the "leopard men," now carefully
examined the body and said it was not the killer of the chil-

dren. The French administrator then demanded that the
fetish priests produce the guilty killers, if the leopard was not
guilty.

The entire village was assembled, and a certain number of
"suspects" were placed on a platform and required to drink
a concoction prepared by the witch-doctors. The purpose of
this was to "smell out" the culprit who had dressed in a
leopard's skin and killed the children. Those who vomited
the concoction would be regarded as vindicated, and anyone
who failed to vomit would die—as proof of his guilt!

"Many of the old timers had been through this sort of
thing before," the French administrator told me. "We
caught them putting their fingers down their throats. Others
had naturally sensitive stomachs. All but two vomited up
the stuff they drank, and these two died shortly afterwards.
The witch doctors immediately pronounced them guilty of
killing the children."

Whether the witch-doctors used actual poison or not is
hard to determine. They drank the stuff themselves, and the
French administrator was of the belief that it was merely a
foul concoction, and was not poison. If so, the men who died
in all probability died of fear, because they had not been able
to vomit the stuff, or perhaps they died of a guilty conscience.

I asked the Prince's permission to talk with one of the
witch-doctors of the famed *vodun,* or "voodoo" cult. This
strange practice of witchcraft, with all its terrifying implications, was brought to America from the "Slave Coast" of
Africa by Negro slaves, many of them from Dahomey. It
flourished for years in Haiti and the British West Indies and
in Negro communities in the United States. It is probably
the most dangerous form of witchcraft known to the natives
of Africa, and the sorcerers who practice it are regarded with
dread by all African Negroes.

One day an old man approached me while I was taking pictures near the entrance of the palace courtyard, and muttered that he would be greatly favored if he could be the "guide" of the visiting "*gris-gris* man." I assumed he referred to my camera equipment, believing it was an important fetish, and that I was the priest of that fetish.

I mentioned that the Prince had provided me with such guides as I needed, but he shook his head violently, and grimaced. I gathered from his patched up combination of Portuguese and a few scattered words of English, French and native dialect, that his mission had the Prince's blessing.

"You see *K'po* convent—no *gris-gris*," he said, pointing to my camera. I understood that he had referred to a meeting place of "leopard men" and that perhaps he would take me there, but did not want me to make a fetish with my camera. I nodded, and followed him to my jeep, which had been brought up from Ouidah. We climbed in and he directed me to a road leading out of the city, toward the hills which rose directly east of Abomey.

On the way I tried to get the old man to explain more fully what he was going to show me. There was no particular danger in accompanying him, yet I was not entirely sure that Prince Aho had approved the trip, and I was not anxious to have anything disturb my cordial relations with Dahomey's ruler.

The old man was named Ngambe; and I gathered that he was himself a *gris-gris* man, at least on a part-time basis. He indicated at the start that he expected compensation for his effort, and I readily fished out some franc notes. In the old days of Dahomey cowrie shells were the accepted currency for all trading except that with outsiders; but this had long since given way to a more modern exchange.

The old man grinned as he pocketed the bills. He was a

thin, tall man with stringy arms and cavernous hollows in his cheeks. His forehead was slanting, with a heavy projection of bone over his eyes, which were dark and brilliant.

He did not mention *vodun* in his reference to the rites I was about to see, although he had referred to the "leopard." Both words are very little used by natives of Africa. But I was sure that was what he meant.

We found the "convent," or temple, deserted. It was a small shed, a couple of miles from Abomey. In front of the shed was a small pot, painted red; and directly behind it was a fairly large tree, with the trunk painted white. Around the front of the shed was arranged in a semicircular row a number of dry palm nuts, each with a strange geometrical figure carved on it. The figures ranged from a circle and crescent to squares and triangles, and even five-pointed stars. I counted sixteen; and later I learned that these are the sixteen signs of the deity, Aho, who represents wisdom.

Above the door of the shed was a hemp rope, to which a number of palm leaves were attached, like a ragged and emaciated stalk of bananas. This was a symbol of *K'po,* the deity of the leopard, which was sacred in Dahomey.

While we watched from a place of partial concealment near the edge of the clearing, a man was led into the clearing. He seemed in an almost intoxicated state, his face turned upwards with an expression on his face that can be most nearly described as pure ecstasy. His thick lips rolled back in a smile, and his eyes were open; but he seemed otherwise unaware of any of the things going on around him. Two men held his arms as he stood in front of the house.

Soon a man came out, wearing the usual tuft of hair on an otherwise shaved head, with a feather stuck through the tuft. I recognized him as the fetish priest. He went over to the pot and sprinkled some powder-like substance in it. Then he took some leaves from a bag that hung around his waist. None of these substances were put into the man's mouth as he stood, held by the two assistants; but slowly his body seemed to become more rigid.

The fetish priest stood for some time in front of his subject. Then a single file of natives came out of the bushes behind the shed and began to dance in a slow, rhythmic trot around the group in front of the shed, turning back and forth like a snake coiling upon itself.

This lasted for several minutes. Then the man who was being treated began to sway, and he was led inside the shed. The two men and the fetish priest soon left, and the dancers followed. It was quite a brief ceremony, and Ngambe explained to me that the man was "ready." I assumed he meant he was prepared for whatever the ritual accomplished. In any event, he seemed to have been well doped up in advance, and when it was over he was evidently in a state of trance.

Again, I had no way of knowing whether this was the result of the administering of a drug; or whether the man was under the influence of hypnosis. As Ngambe explained it to me, this was a method of "cleaning out" the spirits from a man who wanted to get married, so that his children would not have any unwelcome spirits.

The essence of *vodun*—or *tovodun* as it was originally called—is the power of the fetish. Under the control of witch doctors, these fetishes are believed to have complete power over any human in whose body they take up residence.

In the earlier days of Dahomey, the "voodoo" was also known as *akvodun,* which is a worship of the dead. The dead are considered to be in two groups: the ancestors of the living, and others who have died, including enemies. For several months after a man dies, he is supposed to retain his individuality, and even his name; and it is during this period—

particularly if funeral rites are delayed—that the spirit of the
dead man may become dangerous to the living by taking
control of a living person, or his spirit.

The practice of "voodoo" which became so terrifying in
the Western Hemisphere was based upon the control of these
spirits by *vodun* witch doctors, who supposedly use these
spirits for whatever malignant purpose they wish.

In the early days human sacrifice was part of the *vodun*
worship; and even worse, the witch doctors were able to reduce the will of their victims to a form of abject slavery in
which they literally seemed to have been returned from the
grave.

The Negroes of Dahomey have a special form of worship
of the dead. The fetish priest, Ngambe, whom I got to know
quite well during my stay at Abomey, told me the *vodun*
rites were based on the belief that the souls of those who
have died will continue to float around the neighborhood of
the graves and sometimes a soul will enter the body of another living person. In such cases it can do great harm.

The startling thing about this belief is the conviction that
bodies themselves can be used as slaves, *after they are dead*
and the spirit has fled to another place. The witch-doctor
merely contrives a way of introducing his fetish into the body
of the victim who becomes a "soul slave." It was the belief
in this phenomenon peculiar to the "voodoo" cult that convinced the village witch doctors that a bewitched soul had
entered the body of the leopard which killed the two
children.

There are other souls, or spirits, according to Ngambe,
that wander around freely, disconnected from any particular
body; and these can cause harm in many ways, although they
supposedly can be controlled by the fetish priests. Every in-
habitant of Dahomey carries an amulet made by a fetish

priest as a kind of personal insurance against these wandering spirits. Parts of bodies of chickens or domestic animals are often seen in the villages, nailed to the doors of huts as fetishes to protect the family against malignant spirits.

Each fetish has some animal, or a snake, which is the symbol of its power on earth. Prince Aho's symbol was, of course, the leopard. This animal is regarded by the Negroes as among the bravest in Africa, and also among the most cunning; and for this reason members of the "Agassou" are greatly feared and respected.

9

THE RITUAL OF "returning from the dead" is perhaps the most mysterious and least understood of the practices of the "voodoo" fetish priests. I had been in Abomey for perhaps three weeks before I was able, after considerable pressure in the form of the customary symbols of persuasion, such as franc notes, to arrange with Ngambe for a trip to one of these secret ceremonies.

We travelled several miles from Abomey until we found ourselves in a cleft in the mountains, through which the road, little more than a trail, wound downward into a rather steep valley. At the upper end of the valley we came to a clearing. Ngambe cautioned me to be silent, although I was not sure whether this was to conceal my presence or impress me with his efforts to "smuggle" me into the ceremony.

The ritual, as I understood it from Ngambe, was to "return from the dead" a man who presumably had been attacked by the evil practice of a witch doctor from a neighboring village. The fetish priests of the man's own village had gathered to destroy or neutralize the power of the spirits who had "killed" him.

We squatted in a clump of bushes, perhaps fifty feet from a place in the clearing where a group of natives had gathered. I was pretty sure Ngambe had made the "arrangements" by distributing part of the money I had given him among the local men who were to take part in the ceremony. It was late in the day, and although I had brought a camera, I was disappointed that it would be impossible to take pictures because of the twilight.

A man lay on the ground, apparently lifeless. I noticed that one ear had been partly slashed off, but it seemed to be an old wound, and otherwise he bore no mark of violence. Around him stood a group of black men, all virtually naked except for a few who wore shirts hanging loosely at the waist. I observed that several sported the curious head-mark of fetish priests, a tuft of hair in the center of the forehead and the rest of the skull shaved. They made a low hum of voices as they prepared for the ritual.

An old man, wearing a faded brown Army shirt hanging loosely almost to his knees, appeared to be in charge. He spoke fiercely to the others, shaking his finger; and I noticed circlets of flat ivory beads around his wrists. I took him to be the chief priest of whatever fetish was being used in this ceremony.

Several men suddenly stooped and lifted the lifeless figure from the ground, carrying him to the center of the clearing. He was dumped rather unceremoniously on the ground, and it seemed apparent that he was either dead, or very close to it. I wondered if this could be the "ritual murder" which I had heard about in the Belgian country—a phase of witchcraft barred by all governmental laws in Africa.

Two men began to beat on tree-drums made of hollow

sections of logs. The low vibration filled the forest with a
steady rumbling noise that hummed in continuous reverberations of sound. The drummers were young men, apparently not priests. Their muscles were like ropes under
the glistening surface of skin; their faces were rigid, and as
they drummed they moved with a rhythmic intensity that
was almost hypnotic. Their hair was woven in strings, with
strands of red and white beads twisted through the thick
braids.

The chief priest, naked except for his brown shirt and
beads, began to dance rhythmically around the prone figure,
muttering in a low, chanting voice. His shirt flapped in a
ridiculous way, exposing his glistening black rump as he
leaned forward in the movements of the dance, swaying from
side to side with the sound of the drums.

I leaned over and said to Ngambe: "I am white doctor. I
would like to see if the man is dead. Can you fix this?"

Ngambe shook his head violently, but finally he rose and
went forward. There was some kind of conference, and the
old priest stopped dancing to chatter some rather violent re-
marks. The others shook their heads, and finally Ngambe
came back to the bushes where I still squatted.

"You are doctor?" he asked.

I nodded, feeling again that I need not elaborate on the
distinction between my profession of dentistry and other
medical fields. Ngambe signalled to me to follow him.

"Do not touch!" he said sharply. I nodded again, and
knelt down beside the prone man. The dancing had stopped,
and the men were standing around, staring curiously at me.
The man on the ground was a healthy fellow, better than
six feet tall with a deep chest and powerful shoulders and
arms. I worked my position around so that my own body

was between the victim and the others, and I quickly lifted his eyelid, trying to determine whether there was the Argyle-Robinson pupillary reaction. There was none. I also managed to feel his wrist to see if there was any pulse. There was no sign of a heartbeat.

There was an audible noise, like an intake of breath, from the group who had been standing in silence. I turned to Ngambe, and his eyes were glittering with anger; there seemed to be some kind of fear in his expression.

"He will die!" he said to me in French. "You touch him —he will die!"

"He is already dead, Ngambe," I said, standing up. "This is a crime. I must report it to the French police."

Ngambe continued to shake his head, and the old chief priest suddenly resumed his dance around the body. I moved away from the group, wondering what I should do. This was an unusual situation. While I was not particularly afraid since I knew that the fear of arrest by the French police would protect me from any violence, yet there were elements in the affair that I did not understand and which might easily prove dangerous. I recalled the case of the Belgian police captain Major Roelande had told me about down in the Bapende country, who had been killed and cut into several hundred pieces for use as fetishes because he interfered with tribal fetish worship.

The group of about thirty, gathered in a circle around us, began to chant in low rhythmic tones, sounds between a wail and a growl. The sound rose in volume and tempo until it seemed that it would pierce the ears of the "dead" man—and to my utter amazement, that is exactly what it seemed to do.

The victim suddenly threw one arm across his chest and tried to roll over. The cries of the encircling natives rose almost to a scream, and some drummers began to beat more furiously on their tree-drums. The figure on the ground finally twisted over and got his legs under him, and slowly began to lift himself to a crouching position. His eyes, which had showed no pupillary reaction a few minutes before, were now wide and staring.

I would have liked to examine him to determine the strength of his pulse, and to see if there was any indication of the use of a drug. But Ngambe was quite worried about my presence by this time, and he managed to get me out of the circle of dancing men. Later I asked him if the man actually had been dead.

He shrugged his scrawny shoulders, and said: "Man no die. Only spirit kill him. If spirit no longer wish to kill him, he live."

He spoke in his jargon of Kiswahili, French, Portuguese, and a little English; and the gist of what he said seemed to be that the victim of the ritual I had just seen had been made "dead" by a spirit controlled by a fetish priest who was working for an enemy. This spirit had entered the man's body and caused him to become sick and finally to die. However, for a brief time it would be possible for the man's own spirit to return—if the other spirit were driven out. By touching the man with my hands, I had almost interrupted the whole procedure.

My own diagnosis was that the man had been given some alkaloid drug which induced a state of catalepsy or trance, and his body no longer seemed to function. On the other hand, he might have been in a deep hypnotic trance.

The most surprising part of the whole thing, to me at least, was the fact that the man seemed to have been in such a state as to produce no living reaction to any of the usual tests; and he had emerged from that state without the introduction of any drug or stimulation, or even the touch of a helping human hand.

Later I spoke to a French colonial official about the affair, and he merely shrugged and said:

"You have seen something queer. In Africa, many things are queer."

This seemed to summarize the whole business. I found out, through questions I asked various people, that it was not rare for white visitors to be taken to one of these secret rituals, providing they had won the confidence of the fetish priest who made the arrangements—for a price, of course. However, the rituals were not looked upon with favor by the French police, and were carried on through tacit agreement by the police to overlook the obvious illegality of the practice.

The evil that is inherent in such practices, of course, is in the use of drugs or whatever hypnotic power is exerted upon the victim to make him a virtual slave through a process of "brainwashing" not unlike that practiced elsewhere by supposedly civilized peoples of the world. The use of psychological pressure, whether aided by drugs or not, to exorcise spirits of living people, provides an opportunity to control them. How many such cases are perverted to the hideous crimes of the "voodoo" priests cannot readily be determined, since the fear of the fetish priests in itself is an assurance of the secrecy of their practices.

I did not speak to Prince Aho of my excursion to the ceremony of "returning from the dead," and he said nothing —although I had an idea he knew about it. It was shortly after this that I had an opportunity, through the efforts of the Prince, to visit the "Convent of the Leopard." The term "convent" applied to a small cluster of thatched huts, surrounded by thorn hedges and other jungle impediments, where the secret rituals of the various fetish groups are held. These "convents" are so cleverly concealed that unless a guide directs a stranger to the place, he could pass within a few feet of the fetish huts and not see them.

Prince Aho promised me that I would be taken to the "Convent of the Leopard," but he asked that I first visit the museum of relics of King Glèlè, his notorious ancestor, to acquaint myself with some of the background of this mystic cult.

"What you people of the West call natural are often mysteries to us," he told me, with his inimitable touch of humor and irony. "Likewise what is mysterious to you is quite natural to us. Therefore you must try to understand us as a people before you inquire into what you call mysteries."

This made sense to me. So I visited the museum, which included royal umbrellas, scepters and hammocks, and a cannon which fired twenty-five charges simultaneously—a lethal looking piece that had been presented to King Glèlè by Cha-cha da Sousa, who had traded a beautiful slave girl for the piece.

After going through the museum, including a walk across the chamber paved with human skulls which King Glèlè had built for special dances—probably getting his masonry from the thousands of slaves dispatched in the horrid "Annual Custom"—we were taken to the area where the "Convent of the Leopard" was located. A special ceremony was in progress, and I was invited to take a few pictures.

There were several women standing in a small clearing, at the entrance to the "convent." Each wore a veil made of cowrie shells to conceal her face; and they were apparently in a state of trance. I was told this trance lasted three weeks, during which they would remain entirely under the control of the fetish priests. The trance, or hypnotic state, in which these women had been placed was so complete that they could not even perform normal functions of the human body without help.

The method of hypnosis was interesting. I spoke to Ngambe about it and he told me with rather surprising candor that the hypnosis was based on belief. Each woman believed the fetish was entering her body to control her, and submitted without protest to the control of the fetish priests.

There were special drum beats that served as signals or instructions, which the entranced women understood. This was the end of the three weeks' ordeal, the climax of the ritual. Several tom-toms were being beaten with increasing tempo and volume as we came into the compound. The women started, one by one, to utter strange noises, rising almost to a shriek; and then they started to dance.

It is difficult to describe the effect of this dance with words. There was no choreography or form to the dance; each girl seemed to hurl herself into it with wilder and wilder abandon. They would throw their shoulders forward and backward, much like the movements of West Indian dancers. They apparently could not see where they were going. They would bump into each other frequently, and sometimes one of them would fall. Still following the beat of the drums, she would slowly rise and resume the wild, chaotic dance.

Many people from the village came into the compound, until it became a seething mass of people, with the dancers moving wildly through the crowd. Then the drum beat dropped in tempo and sound, and three fetish priests, or witch-doctors, came forward, carrying chickens and a goat. This was the sacrifice which in former days, I was told, required the blood of humans. The blood from the animals was scattered around the yard, sprinkling the ground and onlookers alike.

Ngambe leaned over and whispered something to me, and I caught Prince Aho's eye. He whispered that I was about to see one of the rare sights of Africa—the merging of human beings and leopards. This was the "lycanthropy" about which I had heard.

The chief fetish priest was standing now in the middle of the careening dancers. Lycanthropy is an exchange of identity, in which a man becomes an animal or assumes many of the outward characteristics and habits of the animal. However, the word is often used loosely to refer to the mingling of men and animals, as if they were of the same species.

Prince Aho whispered to me that if an animal came out of the bushes—presumably a leopard—I was not to touch it under any circumstances. Nor was I to leave; if I did this would violate the fetish code and might stir the anger of the leopards.

The chief fetish priest began to sing a low, funereal dirge. He was a fairly tall man, with wrinkled skin that made a lacework of his face; and his eyes were so brilliant that no matter what he did, my eyes were turned almost hypnotically to his. As the pitch of his voice became higher there was a slight stir, like a shiver running through the crowd. A girl came dancing, or rather floating into the clearing. She was absolutely naked, except for a string of cowrie shells draped around her neck and a cord of cowrie shells around her waist.

The drum beat quickened, and the girl began to dance faster. From Aho's gestures, I understood that she was dancing entirely under the guidance of a fetish, and that she could not have danced without that influence. She seemed to glide through the air, her body shining like black satin in the glitter of lights which were firebrands standing like stalks around the clearing. Her body twisted and turned slowly with each graceful shift of movement. At times she seemed to settle to her knees without giving the impression of any weight on the ground.

She was tall and beautifully formed, with strong limbs and arms, wide shoulders and high, full breasts. Her ebony skin flowed in the flickering lights of the firebrands; and above and around her the trees bent over her in an unearthly majesty, so that she seemed to dance in a great ball of dim light.

Suddenly she stopped and looked around. Then she called out some words in a low, musical voice. The drum beat was almost stilled, leaving only a faint reverberation in the air, and Aho tugged at my arm.

"Look!" he exclaimed, in an ecstatic whisper. "Do you see the two leopards walking beside her?"

The moon had risen over the trees, giving a milky glow to the darkness beyond the range of the firebrands. The girl was only a few paces away, yet I saw no leopards.

The eyes of the natives, however, seemed to follow not only the girl but the space immediately around her, as if there were something which they could see, but which was invisible to me.

Aho kept pressing my arm.

"Do you see—there are five more leopards behind her!"

I did not know whether he was in earnest, or was carrying out a practical joke at my expense. But when Aho suddenly said, urgently, "Step back, or you will touch them!" I decided he was not joking. Whatever might be the physical truth of the matter, Prince Aho thought he saw leopards.

The chief fetish priest began to sing, louder than before; and the drum beat grew in volume and tempo. Suddenly I felt as if my eyes had started out of my head. Just beyond the girl, on the edge of the shifting light, I saw the shadow of an animal; and before I had time to express my wonder, a full

grown leopard glided into view. It might have been my imagination; and if it was, I have more imagination than I thought
I had. Two more leopards appeared behind the girl, stalk-
ing majestically across the clearing, and the three disappeared
into the shadow of the trees.

What was more astonishing than anything else—and in a
way, nerve-shattering—was that I distinctly saw that one of
the leopards had a chicken in its mouth.

"You saw them!" Aho exclaimed triumphantly, his pudgy
face turned squarely toward me.

I could not answer. I did not know for sure what I had
seen. If I had been put under a trance through some process
of mass hypnosis, it was a good one, because I felt otherwise
quite sane and normal.

"There are those who say that these animals appear only
to those who have fetish power," the Prince was saying, in a
friendly, almost ingratiating way, as if he would bridge the
gap of my sudden consternation by some amiable chit-chat.
"I do not know how true this is. They are agile animals and
the spirit which brings them among us also makes the girl
dance."

I rubbed my eyes involuntarily. The ceremony was over
and the people were leaving the clearing. A woman had
bumped into a dancer, and I saw her turn suddenly, her eyes
afire, and shout in Bantu dialect: "Keep that woman away!
She is drunk, and if she gets too close she will get her foot
caught in the tail of my leopards . . . Keep her away!"

To this day I do not know exactly what I saw. I think it
was a leopard—or rather three leopards; but if not, they certainly were reasonable facsimiles of leopards.

During my few weeks at Abomey I was able to photograph
many of the ritual dances which still are a part of the social

and religious life of the country. One of these was the "Thunder Dance," which was not directly related to the practices of witchcraft, but was full of many strange implications.

The Prince usually accompanied me to these functions, always carrying a royal umbrella—a traditional insignia of kingly rank in Dahomey. The umbrella was the equivalent of a flag or heraldic banner. It was decorated with illustrations of the courage and grandeur of the kings of Dahomey. The staff of the umbrella was made of bamboo, and was extraordinarily long, so that the umbrella itself, usually of white cotton or silk cloth, stuck up like a flower on a long stem.

The Prince escorted me personally to the "Thunder Dance," which was held in a courtyard of the palace, carrying his royal umbrella to shade us from the blazing sun.

He stood on the steps of the pavilion, his rotund figure of the proportions of a circus tent to protect the Prince hardly shaded by the umbrella which would have had to be alone, and certainly offered little shade for both of us. Each performer came by, making a low bow and finally falling upon their faces and rubbing their foreheads in the dust. Some took handfuls of dust and scattered it over their heads as they departed, and each time the Prince would snap his fingers as a gesture of approval.

Finally, after a tour of the rectangular plaza—where the "Annual Custom" had drenched the paving stones with human blood a century earlier—the Prince took his place on an elaborately carved stool, surrounded by twenty-eight of his wives.

The "Thunder Dance" was an example of the strange rapport that seemed to exist between the primitive practices of

these people and the forces of Nature itself that defies the
logic or understanding of the civilized man, yet is simple and
obvious to the native mind.

A tall man stepped into the dancing area, waving a *sossayabi*—a long dancing stick with a sharp, axe-like head of
polished brass. When he swished this through the air it was
intended to represent lightning. As he began the undula-
tions of the dancing, whirling slowly at first and then with
increasing tempo, the drums beat out a steady reverberation
that was like thunder.

The man finally took the *sossayabi* between his teeth and
began to revolve in the most intricate contortions; and finally
others jumped into the dancing ring with him and began to
turn and twist, even scraping their foreheads on the ground.
The man with the *sossayabi* seemed to be completely possessed as he whirled past the crowd gathered around the
dancing ring, swinging his axe-like club and coming peril-
ously close to some of the onlookers.

The day had been bright and clear when the dance started,
but suddenly I looked up and the heavens were overcast.
The dance continued, with the rumble of thunder quicken-
ing the pace, and the dancers were now shrieking and dis-
torting their faces while they made seemingly impossible
leaps high in the air. I found myself becoming gradually
under the spell of the strange frenzy that possessed them,
and all the while I was aware of the ominous gathering of
clouds overhead, which threatened to interrupt my picture
taking.

Prince Aho seemed to sense my concern, because he leaned
his huge torso close to me and murmured in my ear: "It will
not rain, because we will not permit the rain without the
rain dance."

I was filming as rapidly as possible, to get everything into pictures that I could; but the sky was soon so dark that taking pictures became impossible. The air was hot and humid—well over a hundred degrees; and in the sky there was the distant clap of thunder, mingling with the roar of the drums. I expected to see lightning and then a downpour, but after a second clap of thunder the dance stopped.

The man carrying the *sossayabi* made a final gyration and toppled forward to the earth, almost at the Prince's feet. His thick lips were covered with a fine white foam, and the manner in which he plunged to the ground left no doubt that he was not faking exhaustion. He had literally danced himself into unconsciousness.

The Prince turned to me, his heavy lips wreathed in a smile, and then looked upward at the sky. The sun was shining brightly in a clear blue sky, and all sign of rain had disappeared.

"We do this for our amusement," he said, still smiling. "In the forest it is not so much for amusement—and it is sometimes fatal to the priests when the rain comes with the thunder."

I could not help but think of Lusungu, and her refusal to indulge in the vagaries of weather forecasting. To this day I have no idea why it did not rain, unless Prince Aho was privy to some special meteorological service that I knew nothing about.

One interesting case came to my attention just before I left Dahomey. A chief had been accused some years earlier of killing two wives by the use of fetishes. He was brought before the French administrative Governor of the Canton d'Oumbegame for sentence, and the death sentence was pronounced. A returned French physician, who was sitting in the courtroom with me, rose and asked that the Governor give the matter further consideration.

"It is wrong," he said, "to kill this man for a death he does not regard as a death."

The Governor, obviously an intelligent and conscientious man, asked the French doctor to explain what he meant by his statement.

"Just this," the Frenchman said. "This man does not consider the kind of death that he brought upon his wives as the same death you are meting out to him. He acted according to his nature when he made the fetishes. Punishing him will make no difference in his beliefs, or those of any of his people. What you should do is substitute some other creative action."

The Governor was quite interested; and in the end he turned the chief over to the custody of the French doctor. The latter taught him to carve.

I have today three wooden "masks" carved by this man, and they are amazing examples of what in our civilization would be a psychotic mind, finding an outlet in the work of carving.

One mask is in the form of a man sticking his tongue out at a doctor, who is examining his throat. It is foreshortened, as the doctor would see the face, the upper teeth thrust out, the nose all nostrils.

The second mask shows two entirely different faces, both as to contours and perspective. One is seen from a lower view, showing the left side of the face with the lips curving upward in a snarl, the nostrils distended and the ear far up on the head. The other is a downward view of the right side, showing a placid countenance, with the mouth even and in repose, the eyes downcast—and the ear at the base of the jaw. It is like a mask with a split personality.

The third mask is the enraged face of an insane man—as if the old chief put all his outpouring of an insane mind into this mask.

And most astonishing of all, the old chief lived peacefully, without killing any more of his wives.

10

My friend, Ngambe, provided me with the clearest insight into the deadly parallel between primitive witchcraft and one of the most devilish devices of modern psychology when he said, speaking of the power of the fetish priest over his people: "He not need steal a man's body—he only steal his head."

The parallel between the practice of "voodoo"—which, in a very real sense, is "stealing a man's head"—and the modern-day practice of scientific sadism known as brainwashing could hardly escape even a casual observer in Africa.

Psychological enslavement is as old as anything we know about people. There have always been men who dominated others. But the skilled, scheming practice that invests and controls a human mind, turning it into putty to be moulded to the controlling man's desires, is a contribution to society that is to be credited chiefly to witch doctors and Communists.

For centuries before this instrument of psychological murder was employed in modern psychological warfare, it was common practice among the *vodun* priests and fetish-worshippers of the "Slave Coast" of Africa.

"Brainwashing" is a literal translation of a Korean expression meaning to "scrub the mind." It is not a new practice in the Far East, and was a part of certain rituals among the natives of Borneo. Among the Dyaks, candidates for the *menang,* or priest cult, go through a ceremony that is quite literally described as "brain washing." The purpose, however, is somewhat less malignant than that of the "voodoo" priests of West Africa or the Chinese Reds.

In his book, *The Natives of Sarawak and British North Borneo,* Henry Ling Roth describes this ceremony as follows:

"After a night of incantation, the *menangs* lead the neophyte into a curtained room where, as they assert, they cut his head open, take out his brains, wash them and restore them in order to give him a clean mind for penetrating into the mysteries of evil spirits and the intricacies of disease. . . ."

This process, gruesome as it may sound, is not quite what is meant by "brainwashing" in the psychological sense, however. As a matter of fact, the ritual among the Dyaks actually is carried out symbolically, and in some cases is omitted entirely upon payment of a small fee. It serves to point up one thing that is fundamental in all primitive witchcraft, however: that is that the effect sought by the witch doctor is always psychological and emotional, rather than physical.

Brainwashing, as employed on prisoners of war, is the clearing, or "washing" of the mind to remove obstacles to suggestion or to remove factors of resistance. Under subtle but penetrating pressure, the mind becomes completely responsive to influences that may be exerted upon it.

Sometimes this is accompanied by physical torture, but more often it is purely psychological, stripping the mind of its stamina or its will to resist. A prisoner, for example, may be consistently denied a cigarette. Suddenly the pressure of denial is released; he is given a cigarette, and the result is a slight crack in his defensive armor. The process is repeated in varied forms until his mind gradually breaks down into a state of confusion, and the practitioner is able to take advantage of this collapse and drive splinters of ideas into the wholly pliable mind of his victim. Finally, the victim no longer recognizes which are his ideas and which are those suggested to him by his tormentors, and responds readily to whatever suggestion is made to him.

One of the symptoms of this disintegration, or collapse of mental stamina and will is the desire to "confess"—and here we find once again some of the methods of the witch doctor. Just as suggestion and confession are the tools of modern psychiatry and brainwashing, so are they the tools of the witch doctor. It might be well at this point to outline some of the basic techniques of brainwashing, and see how they compare with the practices of the witch doctor.

Each person's living habits are largely dependent upon maintaining a workable relationship with his total environment. When something happens that disturbs this relationship, his psychological habits are affected. The technique of brainwashing consists largely of taking all these normal living habits and environmental relationships into account, and then bringing unpleasant pressures, such as fear, worry, anger, loneliness, to bear upon each facet of this environmental framework. Sometimes the process is accelerated by physical pressures, such as hunger, fatigue, or tensions induced by direct threats—either to the victim or those close to him. The brainwashed victim is forced into a condition of complete mental exhaustion, confusion and insecurity, until a state of mental sickness is induced in an ordinary healthy mind.

Under these conditions, the victim *wants* to do whatever his interrogators ask him to do, including the confession of crimes he did not commit. This is different from customary police techniques, and it is precisely this difference that is found in the practice of "voodoo." The victim undergoes a longer period of preparation, or conditioning. The fundamental condition is created by the society in which he lives. But the process is the same. He is willing to be enslaved, or to die, if that is the will of the fetish priest. His non-resistance is not the result of pressures, or even beatings; it is the result of faith in the fetish priest and belief in all his miraculous powers. This faith and belief are held by every member of the primitive society.

One of the most difficult things for the sophisticated mind to grasp is the fact that there is no moral code opposing the practice of witchcraft in primitive societies. In most of Africa, South America and Australasia, where I have seen many examples of the practice of witchcraft, I have found only legal opposition by colonial governments.

Even the notion of psychological enslavement is acceptable to the natives of Dahomey and the Niger delta country. As long as these tribesmen can remember, strong people have made slaves of the weak. They have no difficulty in absorbing the idea of "soul enslavement," such as the fetish priests practice, because they have never seen or been part of life in which the strong did not rule the weak. They do not divide things into "good" or "bad," but into that which is powerful or weak.

The missionary's notion that the practice of witchcraft and belief in the spirits and demons that infest the world of the African bar him from an understanding of monotheism, or

Christianity, misses an important point. The primitive peoples of the world ultimately conclude that God has done better by the Europeans than the natives. Therefore the native
turns to the one person who he thinks can help him in his
troubles: his witch doctor.

The Bantu tribes, spreading from Cameroon down to
Angola, believe in an all-powerful god. They use various
names, such as "Mau," "Niambe" or "Anyambe." But they
are convinced God has forgotten them—that He is the God of
the white people, and they must look to lesser deities for
help. There is a Bantu prayer which says: "A Paia Niamba
—have you forgotten your children?" This bears a striking
resemblance to the same desperate cry that has rung down
through the ages: "Oh God, why hast Thou forsaken me?"

This point is brought out not for any significance it may
have in the field of missionary work—in which I disclaim any
authority—but because it points inevitably to a state of mind
in which the primitive patient approaches his witch doctor.
His relationship with the white man's theology—even if he is
a converted Christian—is reduced from the rarified atmosphere of the missionary's preachments to the more practical
demonstrations of the witch doctor, the sorcerer and the
fetish, in which he believes.

When he is sick, he believes a spirit has been sent his way
by a sorcerer, and the only possible remedy for the situation
is to get the help of someone who can chase away the spirit.

The use of physical aids, such as amulets, charms, fetishes
and drugs is a stock in trade of the witch doctor's profession.
One of the astonishing things about the witch doctor's practice is that he can manipulate the drugs or other aids to his
own advantage by psychological means.

Ngambe once showed me a drug, or rather a concoction of
pulverized leaves made of the *akazya* plant, which contains a

powerful drug, which can act either as a diuretic or a nar-
cotic, producing dizziness or even unconsciousness.

"How can the witch doctor possibly control the way in
which the drug will act?" I asked the old man.

"Very simple, sir," he said. "If witch doctor give this to
man who has brought no evil, he make well. If man has
brought evil, he make sick and fall down."

I remembered the strange effect of the poison fed by the
old *ngombo* to Lusungu's ex-client—and the complete lack of
a similar effect, except perhaps the vomiting, when it was
drunk by other people. There seemed to be only one plausi-
ble explanation: If the victim believes he is guilty, and believes that the drug has the power of indicating his guilt, the
drug will ferret him out and perhaps kill him. The effect of
the drug is thus accomplished by psychological means.

One of the significant characteristics in the practice of the
"white" art is the fact that witch doctors who are healers
seldom attempt to cure a sickness which is outside the range
of their supposedly occult powers. My friend, Pimento, the
Indian medicine man, made it clear to me that he regarded
the white man as immune to his healing powers, and he knew
that Indians afflicted with such diseases of white men, as in-
fluenza, syphilis and tuberculosis were not affected by the
ministrations of the Indian medicine man.

When a tribesman is suffering from some disorder, he goes
immediately to the local witch doctor and asks to have the
evil "spirits" driven out. If it is a "spirit" unfamiliar to the
witch doctor, or one he suspects is allied with the white man's
sorcery, he finds a way to dismiss the man or turn him over to
another practitioner.

Once the witch doctor has decided he can undertake the
case, he interrogates the patient, or client, just as a psychiatrist does. He describes the cause of the ailment in terms of

a fanciful world of spirits—a world that is incomprehensible to us, but very real to the primitive mind. The scenes are all familiar: jealousies, evil desires, adulterous desires—all the things that he finds in his everyday world. Fragments of ideas are brought out in the patient's mind, until the witch doctor knows exactly what to prescribe—and knows also that he has a willing patient.

The dance, in various forms, is perhaps the best example of the effect of the weird powers of the witch doctor over his followers. I have seen dancing literally change a man into a form that seemed more animal than human. There is no real physical change, of course; but to all outward appearances the man (or woman) becomes a beast in human form.

I have seen this transformation in the jackal dance, among the Bapende, and in the leopard dance in Dahomey. In each case the actions of the subject who is under the influence of the witch doctor reverts entirely to the animal, even to the sexual excesses that are performed.

When I was traveling in the Bapende country, I spent some time in the village of Niaha Kikessa (which means "small snake") about twenty-five kilometers from Kilembe. I saw several native dances, but by far the most astonishing— and from the viewpoint of this inquiry, the most illuminating —was the *Bunga Bunga,* or dance of womanhood. It is forbidden for men to see this dance, under pain of a penalty that may be a fine, or exclusion from the village for life. It is supposed to be the initiation of young virgins into a secret cult.

In order to satisfy the strictly legal requirements, I paid my fine in advance; and the *lemba* agreed that I could take pictures. The dance is performed in the nude, but in deference to my camera the girls wore brief loin cloths.

A guard of men was posted around the clearing, out of sight of the dance, to keep other men and curious boys away. The girls were taken into an enclosure of bushes and the *pemba,* or mask paint, was pasted on their bodies by the elder women of the sect. There were perhaps two thousand women in the village, but only a few were selected as neophytes for this particular cult. They were not bad looking—full breasted, with smooth bodies and gleaming white teeth. Their eyes were alive with eagerness, apparently in anticipation of the ceremony which inducted them into womanhood.

First a fairly large girl came to the center of the ring, beating a huge tom-tom. Then the girls, each with a rattle in her hand, emerged from the enclosure where they had been "painted." To my surprise they came out on their hands and knees, in a queer, hopping gait, like hyenas.

They came into the ring, and suddenly they were moving in a constant, sinuous rhythm, snapping at each other, now and then rubbing their faces in the red dust or against each other. The movement of the dance became faster and faster, until the neophytes—perhaps sixty or seventy girls—were circling in a constant, sinuous chain that was beautiful and intoxicating to watch. As I saw their faces stream by in the glimmering light, I realized they were completely under the spell of the dance.

Later I saw a more elaborate version of the same dance performed by young boys being initiated into manhood by the rite of circumcision, which is almost universal among African tribes. There were only seven initiates in this group, and they gathered near the village of Kiaha Kakessa just after sundown. There was a full moon in the sky, and it cast long shadows across the weird backdrop of palm trees and white sand. Several large drums were being beaten, sending out hollow reverberations into the night.

The boys were huddled together in the center of a ring of older men, near a fire that had been lighted to heat the drum heads of the tom-toms. They were a scared looking lot, cringing together in their nakedness, their eyes white with fear. Men were dancing around them with increasing frenzy, and suddenly a tall man, carrying a rattle, stepped into the ring. I thought this was the *ngombo,* but he was only the master of ceremonies. He shook his rattle, and a chorus of about twenty male voices began a slow, dismal chant. They would sing three notes and then stop. This was repeated in unison, and the dancers began to follow the rhythm.

Suddenly from the distant bushes came a long-drawn cry. It was high pitched, ending almost in a scream; and whether it was human or animal I never found out. There was something of the eerie quality of a coyote's mating call in the sound. The *ngombo* then stepped forward and announced the names of the seven boys who were to emerge from the ritual into manhood.

There was little sound, only a faint rumble of the tom-toms keeping a low, steady rhythm. The dance is known as the *Kasamalunga,* and the ritual is performed by trained dancers, known as *Bafanzami.* They suddenly appeared, creeping out of the bushes on their hands and knees.

They were grotesquely painted, and completely naked. They wore headdresses of white feathers and their faces were smeared with the white *pemba.* They began crawling slowly around the ring in a weird crouching position.

Finally the *Bafanzami* leaped at the cowering boys, huddled together in the center of the clearing, and dragged them off into an inner enclosure in the bushes where actual circumcisions were to be performed. As they dragged the boys away they struck them and slapped at them, and the other men gathered around howling with such frenzy I thought they were going to murder the boys.

The ritual ended in a maddened melee, with everyone screaming and jumping at each other. The screams of the boys, as they were operated on, were the only elements of reality.

These are forms of the weird rites which border upon "lycanthropy," a form of insanity in which the patients imagine that they are wolves. Perhaps the most startling example of this is the true "jackal dance" which I had the rare fortune to witness in a village near Kilembe.

The dance began—as most of them do—with slow, rhythmic chanting. The witch doctor, or *ngombo,* led the singing and received responses that were like choral responses in a high church service. The tribesmen ringed around a circle, drinking some kind of concoction provided by the *ngombo,* and the rhythm of the drums quickened perceptibly as they drank.

The witch doctor presided in front of a small fire, in which he had brewed a concoction of his own; and he sipped this from time to time from a small wooden bowl. Suddenly out of the silence the faint sound of a jackal's cry drifted out of the jungle. The chanting increased sharply to a shrill scream and abruptly ended with the wailing cry of the jackal floating faintly on the air.

The *ngombò,* who had been crouching on the ground, now moved into a slow dance. He wore a jackal's head as a headdress, and he was draped with jackal skins. His body was painted with white stripes and his ribs were outlined in white. His dance was a slow movement around the inner perimeter of the circle of men, and he stopped from time to time to peer at the faces of the savages around him.

As the dance warmed up, the *ngombo* began a shrill song

that seemed to be a cross between an incantation and a tirade. Then he uttered the shrill scream of a jackal at night; and from out of the forest—possibly from human throats—came screaming cries, one after another, until the night was filled with these wailing noises.

As the jackal cries increased, they seemed to be nearer; and finally I could distinguish the high screams of a female and the growling call of the male. The *ngombo* meanwhile danced more and more feverishly until he fell to the ground, from exhaustion as well as from the effect of the stuff he had been drinking. At this point a small group of men and women leaped into the circle and began to dance.

Now began the horrid part of the ritual. As they danced, they began to growl and finally they fell to the ground and completed the dance on their hands and knees, prowling around each other like animals.

Suddenly a dark form shot into the circle, and at first I thought it was a native dancer. Then I realized it was a jackal. The animal ran through the dancing group, snarling and snapping at both women and men.

The closing part of the dance had indications of an orgiastic relationship—not between the men and women, but between both sexes and the dog.

My friend, the *lemba,* informed me that this was the mating of an old friend, a human in the form of a jackal, with the human dancers.

What was most astonishing to me was that by the time the dancers reached this level of their performance, they *looked like jackals.* And what is even more astonishing, the women later bore the scars of claw marks, as distinctly as if their flesh had been raked by the claws of a mating jackal.

11

DEEP IN THE Ituri Forest, a massive layer of almost impene-
trable jungle which spreads over the northeast corner of the
Belgian Congo, I found perhaps the most unusual, and yet
sensible, combination of the old and the new in jungle medicine that I have ever encountered.

It was here I met "Doctor Totoride" in his jungle habitat.
He lived on the banks of the Epulu River, some three hundred miles east of Stanleyville in an area bigger than New
York State over which a few faint roads carry the only
mechanized traffic. This is the land of the Pygmies, those
small Negroid people who have an unusually friendly relationship with their Bantu neighbors.

I had been told in Stanleyville where I could find "Doctor
Totoride," in his jungle clinic about a mile off the road. His
name in Kiswahili means "Strong Medicine." I had known
him many years before, when he was a young anthropologist
out of Harvard, bound for unknown places in the world to
find out how the primitive people lived.

Now he was established as a jungle doctor, and the Pygmy and Bantu tribesmen among whom he lived for twenty years had "accepted" him. He had been able to team the white man's medicine up with the magic of the native witch doctors. It seemed to me this presented the most unusual opportunity I would ever find of observing this combination being practiced, so to speak, on the same clientele.

I had met "Doctor Totoride" some years before at the Explorers Club in New York, when he was known as Patrick Russell Lowell Putnam. He was the scion of an old Boston family which traced its forebears back to the settlement of Massachusetts Bay Colony, and whose ancestors included General Israel Putnam, the Revolutionary War hero.

Pat Putnam had become a man of medicine more or less as a result of an accident. He was trampled and almost killed by an elephant, and the Pygmies of the Ituri Forest rescued him. They carried him to their village and nursed him back to life again, with the aid of witch doctors. Thereafter he lived among them, devoting his life to giving them medical care in his jungle clinic.

I took the rough dirt road that leads up from Stanleyville, the last deep-water port on the Congo before the river plunges down from its birthplace high in the Central African plateau which surrounds Lake Tanganyika. The road runs from Stanleyville to Manbassa and the Uganda country above Lake Victoria.

The road itself, hacked out of the solid jungle, was a rugged "washboard" and when the jeep in which I was riding turned off into a narrower road marked by a sign reading simply "Putnam," I was glad to be near the end of my journey. Behind the road, cut through the heart of the Ituri Forest, lurked all the hidden dangers and treachery of the jungle; yet at the end of this side road I knew I would find a tall, quiet-speaking man who had in a way consecrated his life to repaying a debt he owed the Pygmies.

The "camp" consisted of a few low, sprawling houses a short distance from the river. About two hundred yards from the main group was a bamboo hut, thatched with leaves and vine tendrils, one side partly open and facing the river. It was under a rough embankment, and looked more like a long shed than an office. I stepped through the wide entrance into the hut, which was about ten feet long and six feet deep, sloping back against the embankment to shed the torrential rains that poured down upon the equatorial forest.

A fairly large table occupied most of the center space; and behind this sat a tall man in a faded blue denim shirt, holding a syringe in one hand. His eyes were upon a Pygmy woman, apparently in a coma, lying on a rattan stretcher.

"How are you, Pat?" I said. "Long time no see."

He lifted his free hand, holding the syringe, and I noticed that the other hand was holding the wrist of the Pygmy woman, taking her pulse. His gesture was one of recognition and a request for silence. He glanced at me and smiled. Except for his blue eyes, which shone out of the cavernous sockets of his gaunt face, he was so blackened by the sun that he might have been taken for a Bantu native or an Arab trader. His hair was close cropped, and he wore a full beard in which streaks of gray were plainly visible.

I waited until he was finished. Then he stood up, still staring at the form of the woman on the stretcher. Except for the sunken cheeks and the beard, he looked much as when I had last seen him at the Explorers Club in New York, many years before.

"Pleural pneumonia," he said, with a kind of helpless wave of his hand toward the woman. "She's on penicillin, but she doesn't react to it. She needs aureomycin . . . I'm waiting for a shipment. The witch doctors got to her before I did, as usual."

He spoke with a bone-tiredness in his voice that made me realize how close to exhaustion he was. It was more expressive than anything he could have put into words. Fifteen years at this "clinic," wasting away under the combined influence of jungle fevers, the rotting dampness of the climate, and the almost hopeless job of caring for the health of several hundred Pygmies had all but done for him.

"She had trouble delivering her baby," he said. "Yesterday they brought her in. Her abdomen was badly swollen and she had a raging fever. She'd given birth while carrying a load of wood to her hut, and the baby was almost two months premature. She'd been afraid to come to me for some reason, and the local witch doctor was treating her."

He shrugged helplessly.

"What's her chance?" I asked.

Pat Putnam shook his head. "Her milk dried up, and she couldn't feed the baby. I think we'll pull the baby through all right, but for her it is probably too late. If that damned aureomycin would only arrive . . ."

He carefully inserted the hypodermic needle into the unconscious woman's arm, removed it and swabbed the tiny blue mark with a pad of cotton. Then he handed the instrument to a native attendant, who stood behind him, dressed in a white hospital robe. He was barefooted, and had the usual tribal markings on his cheeks, but he handled the syringe with professional ease.

Pat Putnam took down a decanter of Portuguese wine from a rack above his medicine cabinet, and poured some drinks. Two Pygmy men, who had been standing near the doorway when I entered, stepped inside and the Negro attendant chattered to them briefly in Kiswahili. The two men picked up their spears and trotted off into the jungle.

"They are going back to the village to report to her husband that she is still alive," he said. "They'll tell the witch doctors what happened, and they'll beat on their drums for a few hours. If she had gotten here a little sooner . . . but they haven't learned that yet. They still think the witch doctors must get in their stuff first—and then if we save her, they get the credit. If she dies, I get the blame."

I sipped my wine, looking at Pat Putnam.

"You always have trouble with the witch doctors?" I asked.

He shook his head again.

"No," he said, surprisingly. "They want to help, and often they do. I help them, too. You see, they have a kind of medicine I don't have."

"What kind is that, Pat?" I asked.

"Faith. These people believe in them. If I could get them to believe in me one tenth as much, I could do wonders for them. But it's always an uphill fight . . . They wait until it is almost too late, before they come to me. Then it's twice as hard."

He stood up and took down a light cotton jacket from a hook.

"Come on up to the hotel," he said. "Office hours are over for today."

The "hotel" was the rambling house on the slope above, with a cluster of smaller huts around it. The main house was a one-story affair, with a large central room and wings in three directions. It was built of hand-hewn logs, thatched with nipa palm; and there was a stone chimney of a fireplace behind the central part of the building.

The entire camp was designated on the map as "Putnam." It was the only place in the Belgian Congo, aside from Stanleyville, named for an American, and it was a tribute of the

Belgian Government to this tall, lanky, unassuming man.
He had given up the family position his people had known
for generations to practice the "strong medicine" of the white
man in a land that had known only the witch doctors' craft
since time began.

The "hotel" accommodated a few travellers passing
through the country, on their way to or from Stanleyville; and
although it was off the "main road," everyone knew about it.
The tourist traffic paid most of the bills of the clinic. The
hotel was run by Anne Putnam, Pat's wife, whom he had
married some years after he first came to the Ituri Forest.

The two operations just about offset each other. The Belgian Government supplied most of the medical supplies, and
Pat's own personal funds, back in Boston, made up the
difference.

The story of how Pat Putnam got into this work—which
ultimately took his life—is quite interesting. He was a graduate of Harvard University in the Class of 1925; and as an
anthropologist, he decided to study some of the aboriginal
peoples of the world at first hand. Shortly after graduating,
he started on a vagabond voyage around the world, and
wound up in Dutch New Guinea, where he found enough
aboriginal life to whet his appetite.

"Once you get the bug, you never quit," he told me. He
had met a Dr. Matthew Sterling of the Smithsonian Institution in Paris; and through him he made a connection with
the American Museum of Natural History, which put him
on the road to the Belgian Congo with an anthropological
expedition. Pat Putnam was assigned to an area around
Paraji, beyond Stanleyville, which was known as the "Weyli
land." When he arrived at the village where he was supposed
to study the Pygmies and learn their language, he found the

village had been deserted—apparently due to the forewarning of his arrival.

He took Abuzinga, a Bantu boy who had come along as his helper, into the brush to see if he could locate any trace of the missing Pygmies, and they ran into a small herd of elephants. The boy ducked into the brush, but Pat couldn't get out of the way of one of the charging bulls.

"It happened so fast, I didn't have time even to think about what I ought to do. The first thing I knew the bull came by me, apparently not worrying so much about me as he was about going some place. His left tusk flicked me in the side and knocked me down."

Pat lay in the tall grass, half unconscious, and bleeding badly from the raking blow of the elephant's tusk. He began to scream for his boy: "Abuzinga! Abuzinga!"

Within a short time a number of small shapes flitted out from the jungle and came across the brush country, Abuzinga among them. They made a stretcher of two poles, thatched across with leaves and vines, and carried him to the village.

"Apparently the fact that I had gotten knocked down by the elephant allayed their fears," Pat said. "They returned to the village immediately afterward. When I asked them later why they had not come when I first shouted, they explained that they thought the elephant had killed me, and it was my ghost shouting.

"Since they believe a ghost only cries once, they knew when I yelled the second time that I was still alive."

Pat had been badly gored in the side and back, and from the loss of blood and fever he soon became so weak he asked them to take him back to the base at Paraji. However, he was too sick to travel, and for three weeks the Pygmy witch doctors cared for him, treating him with herbs and native medicine—and a certain amount of tom-tom beating.

"They did a real job," he told me. "Within a month I was able to get back to Paraji under my own steam."

Pat Putnam returned to the United States where he slowly regained his health. The "bug" hadn't left him as far as his anthropological and personal interests in the Pygmies of the Ituri Forest were concerned; and he studied Red Cross field work in New York and Belgium. He was sent back to the Congo as a "sanitation engineer" on a project of the Belgian Government to build a road through the Ituri Forest from Manbassa, near the Uganda border, to Stanleyville.

He finally settled at a place called Nya Nya, on the Epulu River; and except for a trip to the United States now and then—including one in 1946 when he met and married Anne Esiner, a New York artist—he remained in the Ituri Forest for the rest of his life.

During my stay at "Putnam" I went over the file cards of the various cases Pat had treated—malaria, typhoid, dysentery, dengue fever, syphilis and yaws, among others. There were hundreds of cards, many with diseases not fully understood by our medical scientists of today.

"You mentioned that the witch doctors helped you," I remarked, while Pat Putnam was sitting in his medical hut, going over several cards of cases that were on his list for the day. He nodded; and then he said:

"I've got a woman who will be brought in today on a litter. I've been over to the village and they've decided to let me treat her. But it will take more than medicine to make her well."

My curiosity was aroused. I waited for the patient to be brought in, and in the meantime Pat told me the story of her injuries.

A child in the village had been killed by a leopard. While the "Leopard Society" is not a Pygmy institution and is more active in the areas north of the Congo and the Ubangi, the leopard is a sacred animal even to the Pygmies, probably because of his great fierceness and courage.

Consequently, the witch doctor in the village, who was called in to see the body of the child, and to prescribe the rituals necessary for the parents of the dead child, insisted that it was not an actual leopard but an evil spirit that had entered the body of the leopard and killed the child. When the men in the Pygmy village prepared to go into the bush and track down the leopard, the old witch doctor ordered them not to hunt down the leopard.

He said it was a demon that had taken possession of the leopard, and the demon must be ferreted out. This threw the Pygmies into a state of terror. The demon might be present almost anywhere, and each Pygmy looked upon his neighbor with growing suspicion.

While this panic was developing, the Pygmies remained in the village, and the leopard took advantage of this lull in hunting activities to raid the village. He was attacked by the Pygmies and riddled with their small hunting arrows; but before he was killed, he lashed out at a woman and severely slashed her with his claws.

This was the woman who was brought in that afternoon. Pat cleaned her wounds and stitched them. It was evident that the woman was in great pain, but she did not cry out. When she left, Pat said to me:

"She will get well—and a lot of the credit is due the witch doctor."

I asked him how he figured that, since it seemed to me that the witch doctor had brought on the whole thing by insisting that the Pygmies must not hunt down the leopard. The beast evidently liked the taste of human flesh and would have been a menace to the people of the village until he was killed.

"All that is true," Pat said. "But the witch doctor sent the woman to me. He knew he had made a mistake, and it was his way of saving face. He told her my medicine would cure her. In her own mind, she is as good as well."

"You think the witch doctor will get the credit for the cure?" I asked.

Pat Putnam shrugged.

"That is not too important," he said. "What is important is that she was brought to me in time to do some good. If only a few patients come to me this way, in sufficient time for treatment, it will change the attitude of many others. It will also give the witch doctor a chance to save face—since he sent her to me, instead of keeping her in the village until her cuts were infected. They aren't bad fellows, these witch doctors—and they will work with me if they can do it without losing any of their prestige or personal power.

"The important thing is—I can't work against them. Their people believe in them far more than they will ever believe in me. What I need is cooperation, and this sort of thing helps me to get it."

One day in the Pygmy village we found a woman who had been badly beaten by a group of men and women, one of whom accused her of giving him the "evil eye." She was charged with being a witch, and was supposed to have admitted to digging up bodies and eating the flesh.

Putnam spoke to one of the Pygmy witch doctors, who gave a startling explanation. The woman did not actually eat the dead body, he said; she merely ate the spirit of the dead body. He had told her this, and she readily admitted it.

Again I was struck by the power of suggestion and confession among these people.

A few days after the case of the woman who had been clawed by the leopard, another case came into Pat's medical hut which made it clear to me how vital this rapport with the witch doctors could be.

A Bantu with the Arabian name of Abdul Azizi had gone fishing on the Epulu River, not far from the Putnam camp. He fell asleep on the bank, and was awakened by a sharp pain in his leg. While he slept a crocodile had slithered up the bank and sunk its teeth in his leg. It was trying to drag him down into the river.

He managed to grab a branch of an overhanging tree, and he clung to it, screaming for help. The Bantu men are trained in their youth to fight off a crocodile by jabbing their fingers in his eyes; and the man suddenly let go of the branch and plunged both thumbs into the eyes of the monster. The crocodile opened its jaws, releasing the man's leg and slithered off; and the Bantu painfully dragged himself into our camp.

The Bantu witch doctor advised him that the "strong medicine" of "Doctor Totoride" would drive the evil spirit of the crocodile from his body, and Pat had no difficulty applying treatment, which unquestionably saved the man's leg. Within a few days the danger of infection passed.

Pat grinned wryly when I asked him if he ever invited the witch doctors in for consultation.

"They are not exactly afraid of my 'strong medicine,' which is what they call our treatment," he said. "But they don't understand it. As long as they respect it—that's fine for us. They can bully the Pygmies as much as they like, as long as they let us do our work here—and don't turn the Pygmies against us."

I doubt if there was ever a more effective working arrangement between modern medical science and the practices of primitive medicine than that which Pat Putnam had developed. It had taken him years to win the confidence of the Pygmies; but he had won it, and it enabled him to give medical care to the primitive people whose crude medicine had nursed him back to life nearly twenty years before.

Anne Putnam told me the story of this strange jungle doctor. He had contracted amoebic dysentery on his first trip to New Guinea, and was constantly afflicted with this throughout the years he spent in Africa. He also had a lung ailment, and shortly after he set out with Anne for Africa on a cargo boat, he had to be taken off the ship and returned to a hospital. In spite of his sickness, he returned to the Congo and his jungle dispensary. On one occasion he walked sixty miles through the Ituri Forest to Manbassa to get to a surgeon at the American mission to operate on an infected tooth—and started back the next day!

Whatever it was that drove Pat Putnam to do what he did —in the face of natural obstacles and personal troubles—it certainly was not the gratitude of his patients that inspired him.

"They don't do what I tell them to do, and I doubt if they actually believe I can cure them of their troubles," he told me. "It is only when the witch doctor tells them to come that they will come—and then they are following his orders, not mine.

"The only gratitude they have is for the cigarettes I give them. One fellow came into the dispensary the other day and told me he was sick. I always give them a cigarette when they come for any kind of treatment. Before I could even look at his tongue or take his pulse, he held out his hand and said: 'Me cigarette now!' That's all he really wanted. He may have stuck his finger down his throat to make himself throw up to prove he was sick, for all I know!"

When I left Pat Putnam—and I never saw him again, because he died a short time later from the accumulation of diseases and disorders that had afflicted him for a quarter of a century—I had the feeling that I had seen an experiment in the practical relationship between modern medicine and its counterpart in the jungle that could be duplicated in very few places in the world.

Pat Putnam was neither a missionary nor a social crusader. He was not even a licensed doctor of medicine. Yet he brought science and sorcery together in a strange fellowship —perhaps an actual kinship.

12

――――――◆◇◆――――――

It is a far cry from South America to Africa; and even a farther cry from Africa to the sprawling islands of Oceania and the small continents of the Australasian archipelago. It is half way around the world, in fact. Yet here I found many answers to questions that had first been raised in my mind in the jungles of the Upper Amazon and the dense forests and sunbaked plains of the Niger and the Congo. I had visited the Far East once in earlier years and I returned to it after my sojourn in Africa.

Oddly enough, my first encounter with witch doctoring in Polynesia was with a man who made no pretense of being a witch doctor. He was not even a Polynesian; he was a Frenchman.

His name was Albert Le Boucher, and he was a tavern keeper in Papeete, in the Society Islands.

I had been told about M. Le Boucher by a friend in the Fijis—a remarkable little man named Jokinambu, who went under the title of "Doctor" Jokinambu and was an interest-

178

ing man in his own right. He knew I was looking for witch doctors, and he advised me to see M. Le Boucher, assuring me that he was "the best doctor in the Society Islands—although he is not a doctor at all."

He added, "This man is really much more like the witch doctors you admire so much. He is a healer."

I had met Doctor Jokinambu in Nandi, on the western end of Viti Levu. I was waiting for an airplane, and as I talked with my new friend, I became possessed of a desire to see the French healer he spoke of. He had acquired great fame, not only in the Society Islands but throughout Oceania, by his ability to heal all manner of sicknesses by pricking the skin of afflicted persons with a needle—a gold or a silver needle.

"It is a way of curing that came originally from China," Jokinambu told me. "He may prick the skin on the palm of the hand and it will cure a stomach ache or boils on the buttocks."

When I arrived in Tahiti, I immediately set out to locate this famous French "healer." It was not difficult. Everyone knew him. I found him sitting in the corner of his tavern under a wine shelf. Behind a thin partition was his "consulting office" where he effected his remarkable "cures."

He was a jolly, rotund Frenchman, weighing close to three hundred pounds, and he looked much more like a tavern keeper than a medical practitioner. From what my friend in Fiji had told me of his "practice," however, he might have shaved his head, leaving only a tuft of hair at the peak of his forehead, and amulets and charms scattered around his person, to become a full-fledged witch doctor. But he simply wore a baggy coat and trousers of white drill and an open shirt—the conventional attire for Europeans in the tropics.

From Jokinambu's description of his practice, I believed it consisted solely of auto-suggestion. This bore too much of a resemblance to some of the forms of healing I had seen in Africa and South America to be ignored. I was both curious and skeptical when I went inside the tavern to meet the doctor-proprietor.

He had taken time off from his practice to sip a glass of wine, his great bulk eased against the round framework of the lightly constructed building. His sharp little eyes twinkled as he lifted his glass at my introduction.

"So you have come to prove the great Boucher is a fake!" he said, genially. "Have a drink of wine with me before you do so!"

He winked broadly, and inclined his head with a massive roll toward the bamboo barrier which separated his inn from his office.

"You must be prepared to argue against these people. You see, they are waiting for the great Boucher."

Most of the patients waited in the bar room for their appointments, and I could easily see the economic resourcefulness of the old fellow. He charged nothing for his "treatments," but the business which he realized collaterally must have been enormous. In addition, each patient brought some token of gratitude—a basket of fruits or vegetables, or a jar of fish oil. One girl held a small pig in her arms, and it was kicking and squealing, adding to the general noise.

After we had enjoyed a drink, Le Boucher rose and signalled for me to follow him into his office. He spoke fluently, in excellent English; and he explained as he led me into the small room where he performed his cures, that his love of people rather than his regard for the ethics of the medical profession caused him to omit charging a fee.

"These are my people," he said, waving a fat arm at the crowd of dark-skinned people, many of the women clothed in the flowing and gaily colored dresses that had been styled for them by missionaries. "I love them. The Boucher lives to make others live."

He spoke sententiously; yet the easy flow of his words and the jovial smile seemed to lend an air of light sarcasm to what he said. I judged at the time—and I found out later I was not far from the truth—that Albert Le Boucher was neither a quack nor a man of charity. He lived this way among the people of Tahiti, practicing his curious "cures" and selling spirits in his tavern, because he preferred it to any other way of living. He was a man of considerable self-indulgence who practiced no spitefulness or envy upon other people.

He talked as he worked. A patient was brought into the office and seated in a chair. Le Boucher questioned her gently about her symptoms. She had a pain in her back.

"It may be kidney trouble, doctor," he said, turning to me, "or it may be something else. We shall see!"

He took her hand and seemed to feel her pulse. But he was not content to feel the girl's wrist. He placed his index finger first on the back of her hand, then on her forearm. Then he tried it halfway up her arm, and finally put his finger on the back of her neck.

"She has six decipherable pulses," he told me. "The theory of my cure depends upon a correct analysis of symptoms, based on a study of the pulses. First I talk with the patient to see what organ seems to be affected. Then I must feel the pulse and make my decision."

He pointed to an illuminated chart of the human body, hanging on the wall. There were arrows pointing to the location of scores of "pulses," each corresponding to various ganglions of the nervous system. Each ganglion had a number which was listed at the bottom with a footnote, explaining which organs were affected.

Le Boucher grunted as he tapped a few more "pulses," and then he took out a long silver needle from a black case. He studied the chart for a few seconds, then inserted the needle into the back of the girl's arm. Apparently it was not painful. The girl's face, which had been somewhat set with the pain from which she evidently had been suffering, appeared to relax when he withdrew the needle. Suddenly she was smiling.

"You see—she knows her trouble is being cured!" he said, with a note of pride in his voice. "I have found the identical pulse in her arm which corresponds to the pain in her back. It is a very precise science."

I noted that he had sterilized the needle and swabbed the place where it was inserted with alcohol. Otherwise the entire operation could have been performed in a jungle—so remote was the "cure" from any scientific theory of disease. Yet Le Boucher assured me the "cures" were not transitory.

I asked him, while the next patient was being brought in, how he decided what kind of needle to use—gold or silver. He laughed with a booming roar.

"If the organ is to be sustained—that is, permitted to function in its existing state—the gold needle is used. If there is a state of malfunction which must be relieved, I use the silver needle."

He treated eighty-six patients that afternoon while I sat, alternately poring over his textbooks and watching the practice. I observed that there was considerable pressure applied at times to the place where the pulse was felt, and I recalled some of the stories I had heard about the trick of pressing on nerves to effect certain stimulus, inducing a specific reaction. In some cases this reaction was similar to shock treatments for mental cases.

Once I had witnessed a Japanese jiu-jitsu bout, in which

one of the contestants was able to send his adversary tumbling to the floor simply by pressing sharply with his thumb against the base of the man's ear. I wondered if the application of pressure to one of M. Le Boucher's mysterious "pulses" might not have something to do with the "cures." There seemed to be no relation between where he inserted the needle and the location of the pain, according to any structural physiology I had ever studied. During the afternoon he stuck the needle into a boy's toe to cure sores on the scalp. I happened to follow this particular case, and in about two weeks—whether from the needle or some other psychological cause—the sores disappeared.

Le Boucher's technique, which is called "acupuncture," was not original with him. A Dr. Leon Vrignaut had first brought the technique from China, and Le Boucher—apparently reasoning that an innkeeper might stick a needle into a patient as well as a doctor, provided that he observed certain practices of sterilization—undertook to establish his practice in Papeete. According to the best information I could get, he had been healing patients afflicted with various maladies since 1933.

The fact that he did not charge for his services undoubtedly contributed to the number of his clientele. But soon his name became famous in the Society Islands and elsewhere.

Two other Frenchmen, Dr. Roger de la Fuye and Dr. George Soulie, made a study of this strange art and wrote books on it. These were the texts in Albert Le Boucher's office, to which he frequently referred. Apparently the technique is more effective in places, such as Tahiti, where the credulity of the patient is somewhat greater than in more civilized and cynical parts of the world.

The curious experience with the Tahitian "healer" obviously is not part of the practice of witchcraft. Yet after watching Albert Le Boucher perform, I wondered exactly wherein it was different. He used a physical means of attacking the disease, and he referred to it as a disease, not an evil spirit. Yet there was no ascertainable physical relationship between the disease itself and his means of curing the disease.

One young girl came to him complaining of headaches. Le Boucher said the trouble was with her stomach, which was not an unreasonable assumption. The girl thought the trouble was with her eyes. The needle, however, was inserted in the back of her hand—where Le Boucher found a "pulse" —and within a couple of hours her headache disappeared. Ten days later I checked with the girl, and she had had no recurrence of the headaches.

When I spoke to Le Boucher later, after I had a chance to make certain personal observations on the success of his treatments, he said: "I am not a physician, as you see. Neither am I a charlatan or sorcerer. I have been able, with God's help, to alleviate a great deal of suffering."

There may not seem to be a close parallel between the practice of this genial Tahiti tavern keeper and the witch doctors of Africa, South America or Australasia that I have encountered. Yet I found an intriguing similarity in my own reaction to both kinds of practitioner. Le Boucher's treatments, to be successful, required that his patients have faith in him. Faith was an integral part of his "science," just as it is for the magic of the witch doctor.

The South Pacific is a little world of government officials, international floaters, traders, beachcombers and "islanders." The life of the place revolves around stories and rumors; and the spaces between such remote locations as the Society Islands and the Philippines and Java seem to shrink in this atmosphere of gossipy neighborliness. It was not before I saw

Doctor Jokinambu again, and I told him of my experience
with his healer.

"Did you learn anything from him?" he asked me. I shook
my head.

"Nothing scientific; nothing I could put my finger on—
such as a pulse," I said. "But he has aroused my curiosity.
I am going to dig into this and see what is behind it."

My friend smiled indulgently.

"If you have merely acquired curiosity about this," he
said, "you have learned something." He paused, and then
added: "If you really wish to have your curiosity aroused,
you must visit some of the better *dukuns* of Java, particularly
in Bali. Your friend, Le Boucher, deals with the mind, but
these doctors deal with the spirits."

A short time later I had occasion to recall these words.
I was in Manila, sitting at the airport bar waiting for my
plane. I was on my way to Java, as a matter of fact; and
from there I had planned to go on to New Guinea.

A young fellow was sitting alone at a table; and since the
bar was crowded I asked him if I might sit at the table with
him. He nodded in a preoccupied way, and at first I thought
he was simply being rude. Then I noticed he was staring,
with a kind of fixed intentness, at his glass, as if he would
read his fate in the amber color of whisky and soda.

"Any trouble?" I asked, as I sat down. "Anything I might
help with, that is?"

He glanced up, and for the first time seemed to take cog-
nizance of my presence.

He appeared to be a Dutchman, and later he confirmed
this. He was dressed in the usual white drill of tropical
places. His hair was light and thin, and his eyes a sharp, almost icy blue color. His complexion was the smooth, khaki
color that often is found among blonde people in the tropics.

"I guess not," he finally said, and began to sip his drink.

"If it's passport trouble, perhaps I can help," I said, with what might have been considered unreasonable persistence —but I was frankly curious. "I've been around a lot, and I know the ropes."

The young man shook his head.

"The heat," he said, despondently. "It is driving me crazy!"

It was hot; but this hardly seemed to be an adequate reason for the morbid concentration I had seen on his features. He evidently had lived in the tropics, and should have been used to the heat.

I introduced myself, and told him I was a globe-trotting doctor with a penchant for sticking my nose into other people's business. He managed a small smile, and suddenly his eyes became eager.

"A doctor!" he said. "Perhaps you can help me."

I quickly disclaimed any practicing knowledge of the usual run of maladies. I was a specialist, I said—on teeth. He shook his head, and his despondency seemed to return.

"I guess there's nothing you can do," he said. "I think I'm under a spell. It is the *guna-guna!*"

This was a rather startling statement from such a sedate-looking European. I asked him if he would like to tell me about it, and he told me this strange story.

He was about to return to his home in Holland. He was a hotel man, working as a clerk or assistant manager in hotels in Java. He had worked six years at a hotel in Jokja, and hated it there—mostly, he explained, because of the "deceitfulness" of the place.

This "deceitfulness," it developed, was largely confined to one person—a girl. Her name was Sadja, and she was a Javanese of the higher class, even though she chewed betel nut and therefore had dark teeth. He had fallen in love with Sadja, who was young and beautiful. This was a catastrophe for a white man of good connections. He obviously could not bring her to his hotel, so he went instead to her home. Here he met her uncle, who was a *dukun*.

A *dukun* is the Javanese version of a witch doctor. He can put victims under a spell, which is called *guna-guna*. This may vitalize waning sexual propensities, heal the sick or the lame, or kill an enemy. One of his methods of casting spells or invoking evil spirits is to secure a part of the victim's body —a lock of hair, or a fingernail clipping.

One day my young Dutch friend, who had learned of the *dukun's* techniques, had just come out of a barber shop in Jokja, where he had had his hair clipped. He saw Sadja's uncle dart into the place and snatch some hair off the floor. My friend, curious and a little worried, went back to the barber and asked him whose hair the old man had taken.

"Yours," the barber said. "Watch out for him! He is a *dukun* . . ."

A day or so later Sadja came to his hotel and told him she was going to have a baby. The young man told her he had no intention of marrying her. It was the usual custom for a Javanese girl in such cases to adopt the child into her own family.

Later the girl came with her uncle, and my friend said he had to have the uncle thrown out of the hotel, to avoid scandalous gossip. The uncle shook his fist at him, and threatened him with all sorts of terrors.

Several days passed, and nothing happened. Then my friend saw the girl and her uncle enter the hotel, and he attacked the old man. It turned out to be a case of mistaken identity; he had assaulted a prominent Dutch official who had come into the hotel with his daughter.

Since the young man had no reasonable excuse for the assault, he was asked to leave the hotel's employ, which he promptly did. He was about to return to Holland.

"The strange thing about it," he told me, "is that every time I see a man with a girl, I think it is Sadja and her uncle."

I asked him to look around the bar room and see if he saw anyone resembling them. He shook his head; and then suddenly he pointed to an American Army officer and a young lady, sitting at a table.

"Look!" he exclaimed. "That pair—don't they look like Javanese?"

I might have dismissed this as a case of hallucinations brought about by any one of several forms of mental illness. There was nothing particularly inexplicable about the case —except the young man's apparent rationality on other matters. Later, when I was in Jokja, I checked the young man's story. No one there thought he was insane. They merely thought he had lost his temper and attacked the Dutch official.

Certain other experiences I had in Java, however, led me to review the case in a somewhat different light . . .

I was walking along the market place in Djakarta, the capital of Java, listening to a young, well-educated Indonesian sub-official, who was acting as my interpreter and guide, tell me about the *dukuns*.

He said they use a great many drugs, such as are obtained from herbs and the bark of trees. These are sometimes well-known for their healing powers, but more often there appears to be no curative qualities in the drugs.

"The *dukuns* place great faith in these remedies," my guide said. "They have proven efficacious in the treatment of stomach disorders, insect bites and infected wounds. They do not place much value on the chemical qualities of the drugs, however. It is the supernatural power of the drug they believe in."

We passed a stall where a little old woman was selling these herbs and drugs. In most cases they were sold with glass beads, which—with the drugs—would cure skin eruptions, enable the owner to recover stolen goods, or recreate sexual sufficiency. Some of the charms and amulets that went with the drugs were red lizard tails, used for the cure of leprosy; little white flowers, which would bring on sleep; the sex organs of a crocodile which, in the opinion of the *dukuns,* would rejuvenate old men, particularly if hung over the nuptial bed of an old man who married a young girl.

My guide asked the old crone if she could direct us to a *dukun.*

"She is clever," he told me, in English. "She sells poisons made from poisonous fish and reptiles. Sometimes these bring on the death that the natives attribute to *guna-guna,* which is the spell of the *dukuns.*"

I recalled what my young Dutch friend had said about the *guna-guna* and its evil effect, and I asked my guide if he would explain this practice.

"Indeed," he said, "you may visit a *dukun* if you wish."

He explained that since "mixed marriages" had become prevalent in Indonesia, a large mestizo class had formed that was shunned by the whites and the natives alike, and the normal life of the villages was not open to them. These were reputed to employ the *dukuns* to practice *guna-guna,* and no one could actually tell how much of the evil and even murder accomplished by these "black" practitioners was due to such physical agencies as poison or drugs, and how much was mental.

The Government, he said, had made earnest efforts to

stamp out the practice, yet it flourished and spread its sinister influence among the Indonesians.

"How can you arrange for me to see one of these *dukuns,* if it is illegal?" I asked.

He indicated the old crone, who was pawing among her vials and herbs, evidently trying to find some trinket that would amuse us and make a sale.

"She will find one for you," he said. "I could not prevent it if I wished. Mainly, the effort of the Government has been directed along the lines of education. We hope to stamp out the worst practices this way. Where the agency used is the power of suggestion, there is no way we can reach the source of evil."

It appeared that the drugs used by these *dukuns* were designed primarily to weaken or corrupt the moral strength of the victim, rendering him susceptible to suggestion.

This bore such a startling resemblance to the results—if not the methods—of brainwashing and its African counterpart, *vodun,* that I could not help wondering how widespread this strange knowledge of the techniques of "psychological warfare," common to so many parts of the world, might be.

I began to understand the malady which had afflicted the young Dutch hotel clerk I met in Manila. He was probably a victim primarily of his own imagination; yet the fact that he had visited the home of the girl, Sadja, with whom he was in love, indicated a strong possibility that some kind of drugs, perhaps concealed in his food or in a native drink, might have assisted in the process of reducing his resistance to these suggestions. The fact that he seemed to see the old man and his niece so plainly—even to the point of attacking people under the influence of this distorted imagination —would indicate that the force guiding him was stronger than simple suggestion.

This combination of physical and psychological weapons

by the Indonesian witch doctor made it exceedingly difficult to penetrate the mysteries of their practice. Certainly their hold on the native and half-caste populations was tremendous. My guide told me the story of the "bamboo revolt" in the village of Parakan, where an old *dukun* who claimed to be the most powerful of all *dukuns,* persuaded the people that he had the power to mix a potion which, if applied to the tips of bamboo spears, would make the bearer immune to Dutch bullets.

This was after the end of five years of Japanese occupation, during which all rifles in possession of the natives were confiscated. It seemed like a heaven-sent opportunity to resist the Dutch. The people from surrounding areas swarmed into Parakan on wagons and bicycles and afoot, carrying sharpened bamboo poles. Thousands of these marched against the Dutch, wildly charging the entrenched soldiers, and were mowed down by Dutch machine guns and tanks.

The few who escaped bitterly denounced the *dukun* as being in league with the Dutch; but he was not removed from his position of power in the community, largely because the natives were still afraid of his powers.

When he was brought to trial finally by the Dutch themselves, it was impossible to find an accusing witness against him—perhaps the most significant testimonial to the power of these native beliefs over the credulous people.

In an unguarded moment my guide admitted that he, himself, had been advised by a *dukun* in Jokja to marry a certain girl. I asked him if he had reported the *dukun.*

He shook his head, and grinned.

"No," he said. "I married her. She is now my wife."

It was more or less by accident, a few days later, that I met the *dukun* who had advised the young Dutch official.

13

In the shop of a curio dealer in Jokja, where I went with my guide, I purchased some sarongs which I intended to take back with me as gifts. An extremely pretty half-caste Javanese girl waited on me. She had a small, well-shaped head, with a clear skin and the slightly slanted, dark eyes typical of the Eurasian. She told me she had been studying English, but that her tutor, a young man from Canada, had recently been acting so peculiarly that she was fearful of taking further lessons. Her name was Nusona.

When I returned to my hotel, a young man followed me into the lobby.

"I beg your pardon," he said, touching my arm. "Didn't you just buy something from Nusona, at the curio store?"

I admitted, with some surprise, that I had. He nodded eagerly.

"If it is not too presumptuous, may I ask your advice?"

It quickly developed that he was the teacher of English whose conduct with Nusona had been "peculiar." He said he had fallen in love with the half-caste Javanese girl, but she had spurned his advances, and he was at his wits' end to know what to do.

My guide, who had been listening, tugged my sleeve.

"Take him to a *dukun*," he said. "I'll get you to the old lady who advised me. No harm can come of it—and it will be your passport to see her, if you still wish to pursue your inquiries."

I was rather astonished at this unusual cooperation; but as I have said, I had become used to the unusual. I turned to the young man and asked him if he would like to consult one of the native practitioners. His eyes lighted up.

"I hadn't thought of it!" he exclaimed. "It's a ripping idea! Will you go with me?"

I said I would, feeling inwardly rather ashamed of myself. It seemed to me I had struck a new low in my quest of the secret of the witch doctor's craft—guiding a love-sick youth into the clutches of a practitioner of the "black art." I was also secretly a bit worried. I knew of some rather strange results that had come from a white person's sometimes senseless efforts to penetrate into the mysteries of native witchcraft, and I had a vague and troubled feeling that I might be mixing in something that was not only none of my business, but which I might not be able to understand or control.

Nevertheless, I had made the offer; and so we found ourselves setting out in a drizzling rain on foot, headed for the native section of Djakarta where the guide told me the *dukun* lived.

The young Canadian insisted on going afoot, so that none of the native carriers could go back to Nusona with the gossip that he had visited the *dukun*. After about fifteen minutes plodding along a narrow, muddy road, threading ditches half-filled with slime and intersected by a sloppy cross path,

we came to the alley where the *dukun* lived. By this time
a crowd of children were following us, presumably looking
for bakshish; and with dogs barking at this unusual cara-
van, headed by two white men, it was evident that if Nusona
had any friends in the neighborhood, she would be pretty
well informed of our movements.

We turned into the narrow path that led down the lane,
with piles of refuse along the edge, and finally came to a
small palm-thatched hut with a tiny verandah, which resem-
bled the house we were seeking.

It was set back of a small quadrangle, cleared in the center
as most of the native compounds were, and ringed around
with a collection of huts, like a tiny community within a
community. An old woman came to the door, and waved us
in. She appeared to be used to these visits.

Her name was Gemplakanapos, and she was well known to
many Europeans and Americans who came to Djakarta. She
had a rather finely featured face, with deep-set, jet black
eyes; and although her face seemed tired and worn, she spoke
with a soft, almost caressing tone. I could not understand
what she said, although my friend, the Canadian, understood
her. We entered a small, low-roofed sitting room, followed
by an old man. There were no windows in the room, but
light sifted through the palm-thatched walls, giving the interior a dimly lit, almost eerie, appearance.

My friend explained his problem in the woman's native
language. She asked a number of questions, and I could
gather from his gestures and a glance at me now and then,
that he was explaining the duration and extent of his in-
fatuation. Finally she asked for a guilder, and handed it to
a small boy who came into the room at her call. He went
out and returned a few minutes later with a banana leaf,
some jasmine and frangipani blossoms—two large white flow-

ers and two buds; and also two red flowers, known as *melati*, with two buds. She looked these over carefully, and then set them aside.

She left us and went into another room, walking with an almost stiff erectness surprising in a person of her years. After a short time, my companion began to fidget, and I was not feeling particularly comfortable myself. An odor, something like formaldehyde, seemed to emanate from the room into which the old *dukun* had gone.

After about a half hour of waiting, we saw the old *dukun* come through the door, or opening, walking very slowly. As she parted a cloth curtain that separated the rooms, a vapor came out of the room. It had a heavy odor, a mixture of the smell of an embalming room and incense.

She walked over to a chair, still stiffly erect, and then slowly sat down. Her eyes did not seem to focus on anything, and she began to mumble something. Her voice rose, until it was almost a harsh scream. I suddenly realized that I was feeling the effect of the vapor, or fumes. It was a light-headed sensation, half exultation and half nausea. The old lady's face remained stiff and expressionless, with her lips parted in a grimace that might have been a smile.

I wondered vaguely if the incense contained any of the drugs that cause disintegration of the will and non-resistance to suggestion that my guide had spoken of. I shook myself physically, and tried to straighten a little in my chair. I looked at the young man beside me, staring rigidly at the old woman.

"This is obvious fakery," I thought. "The old woman is a quack!"

Nevertheless, I said nothing. After a while the old woman picked up the two white buds and one red flower, pressed them into a compact shape, and then sewed them into a piece of cloth. She handed this to my friend. Later I learned that she had advised him that he must keep these flowers with him at all times, except when he was in the company of a woman other than Nusona. The other flowers were wrapped in a newspaper, and were also given to the young man. They were to be dropped in front of the door of Nusona's house, so she would step on them when she emerged.

The old *dukun,* Gemplakanapos, then told the young man something that was striking in its simplicity.

"The girl will know that you have come to me. She will see the flowers and will become alarmed. Out of fear she will come to me. I will tell her she must return your love or she may have an evil *guna-guna.*"

She spoke in Javanese, which was later translated for me. The astonishing part of what she said was its completeness. It was entirely up to Nusona—and her imagination. Like so many phases of witchcraft, this was accomplished entirely by the power of suggestion.

Her last admonition was to be patient. He must not go to Nusona, or even see her, until the charms had an opportunity to work on her. As we walked back along the dirty alley and the path that served for a road, I was conscious of many faces peering at us from doorways of huts along the road.

At the hotel in Jokja, the young Government official who had been my guide listened to the story of the Canadian's visit to the *dukun.* He shook his head gravely.

"I am not sure I can advise you what to do," he said. "In my case, I merely asked the old lady out of curiosity, and she advised me. I would have been married anyway—and besides, no racial complications were involved. In your case, the old lady has begun something. Perhaps she cannot stop it."

"What do you mean—cannot stop it?" I asked. "Do you actually believe in this kind of thing?"

"It is not a question of what I believe," the young official said. "You have started a series of things that concern other people's beliefs. Perhaps I should not have advised the young man to go to the *dukun*, but I knew that you, Dr. Wright, wanted to talk with one, and I thought this would be a good opportunity. You see, the native residents will know he went to the *dukun*, and the girl will know. If he places the flowers at her doorstep, the rest of the people will stay away from the place out of fear. They do not want to be contaminated by a witch's spell.

"If he does these things and fails to marry the girl, the family will be ruined socially. She may become an outcast, or the other members of the family may employ a *dukun* to retaliate against him. He will have started a chain reaction, and there is nothing that can be done to stop it."

My schedule made it necessary for me to return to Djakarta and leave for Bali before my Canadian friend had made his decision whether or not to continue with his strange courtship.

Later I returned to Djakarta and saw the young Government official. I asked him what had been the outcome of this curious affair. He told me, and while I was somewhat astonished at the outcome, I was also relieved.

The young Canadian had not taken the flowers to the girl's place and strewn them on her doorstep. But she knew of his visit to the *dukun;* and she herself had gone to the old woman. This much was known. Suddenly the young Canadian became seriously ill. His condition grew worse, and he returned to Djakarta. His physician could find no reason for his illness.

It was learned that the girl, Nusona, already had a husband. He had returned to Jokja from Djakarta while the

abortive suit of the young Canadian was being pressed, and
he also had consulted the *dukun*. Whether Mme. Gemplakanapos was playing both ends against the middle, or merely
wanted to teach the young man a lesson, I could not determine.

But regardless of her motives, my young Canadian friend
had become progressively worse, with no clear indication of
what could be done to make him well; and finally the government official, who had taken a personal interest in his case,
had him put on the boat for Singapore.

"That *dukun* meant business," he told me, rather crypti-
cally—since I was not sure what the *dukun's* business was,
or even whom she represented. "Our young friend was
lucky to have escaped."

He let me have this information for what it was worth,
and I immediately saw the parallel between the Canadian
youth and the hotel clerk from Holland who had the hallucinations of seeing his jilted sweetheart and her uncle in
every hotel lobby and bar he visited.

It seemed to me the *guna-guna* had a habit of reaching
into the lives of white men who transgressed its mysterious
laws; and where primitive belief did not exist, some kind of
sickness took its place.

From Java to Bali there is a shift in religious perspective.
The Javanese are Moslem; the Balinese are followers of the
Hindu faith. The Balinese believe the body possesses certain
magic "charges," like a storage battery, called *sakti;* and that
health and sickness, sexual sufficiency and the reverse, or
even good and bad luck are largely influenced by these magic
charges. Nature has the power to endow anyone with this
magic energy, but only those who live by the laws of nature
receive enough of her bounty to become fortunate and

healthy. Since this magic power comes from nature, it follows that it exists in symbols of nature, such as trees, flowers, and even caves and rocks, all of which possess their powers for good or evil.

The priests, or witch doctors, have established themselves as the people who can direct and control these powers. Anyone wishing to hurt an enemy will consult the witch doctor. He may conduct his practice in a temple, amid ceremonial splendor; or he may do it in more lonely places, brewing magic potions, burning incense and going into a trance.

One of the strangest personal experiences I have ever encountered took place during this visit to Bali. I have not yet been able to explain it, even to myself.

I met one of the local chiefs, Tjakorda Agung, or "Jokorda," as I called him. He was the son of a former Rajah of Ubud, and was a highly intelligent and gifted man who had been educated in a Dutch university. He lived in the center of the island, and had made every effort to preserve the culture and art-crafts, as well as the traditions, of old Bali. He introduced me to his uncle, Ida Bagus Gede Agung, an old man with many talents. He played the flute and the violin, was an excellent sculptor and an architect, a priest and a healer. He was the equivalent of a witch doctor in Java, or in Africa or South America.

This old priest told me there were two kinds of magic in Bali: the *penigwas,* which was magic of the left, and the *penengens,* or magic of the right. The first was associated with evil and death, the latter with healing. Old Agung had a degree in chemistry and had studied with Dutch physicians; yet he believed in amulets and charms. His classifications of magic reflect the almost universal recognition of a distinction between "black" or evil and "white" or good powers.

My friend, Jokorda, translating for me, told his uncle I had two questions I wished to ask him, to test his powers of prophecy. The old man bowed slightly, and led the way into a small square temple in the village of thatched houses. A raised platform was in the center of the single room of the temple, and around it were wooden statues of Balian and Hindu deities, including the four-bodied Shiva and Vishnu.

My two questions were these: "Has anything important happened at my home during my absence; and what will happen to me of importance during the next year?"

The old priest looked steadily at me for some time, then he bent over a vessel in which incense was burning. He pressed one finger against one nostril, and drew in a deep breath, which he held for some time. Then he transferred the finger to the other nostril, and exhaled. It was as if he had circulated the fumes of incense through his head. He did this several times, until suddenly he gasped and his body stiffened and his eyes seemed to roll back in his head.

After a while, his eyes became normal again and he once more looked steadily at me. He spoke in Balinese, and Jokorda translated.

"About your first question, he is able to tell you this much: You live in a large city, near a large body of water. You are not married, but you have two brothers and two sisters. They are well. However, one of your brothers has a daughter, and since you left home she has married. You will find one great change when you return; you have no home to go to."

He spoke to the priest again, and once more translated:

"As to the second question, my old uncle tells me that you will come very near death in the coming year, but you will survive. You have trouble with your eyes, and you must guard them well. That is all he is able to tell you."

I asked Jokorda about payment, and he said I might leave

a gift for the temple. I had taken down Jokorda's words, and after we left the temple, I considered the answers the old priest had given. I had two brothers and two sisters, as he had said. I had not discussed my family affairs with anyone in Java or Bali, and he did not know what questions I had intended to ask; nevertheless, he might conceivably have known these things in advance.

The statement about my niece's marriage was something I knew nothing about. When I returned to my hotel, I asked the clerk to put through a telephone call to my brother, Dr. Louis W. Wright, in Philadelphia—which was my home, and which might be regarded as a "large city near a large body of water," if geography were stretched just a little.

The result of my telephone call left me with a strange sensation of having dipped into the seas of a new and odd kind of knowledge. Everyone in my family was well, but my niece had been married—just recently—to a young Army officer.

It was also true that I no longer had a home. Before leaving Philadelphia, I had made plans to move into a new apartment building and had given up my lease and had arranged to have my effects moved into the new building. It had not been completed on schedule, however, and all my effects were in storage.

This caused certain apprehensive feelings on my part with respect to the rest of the prophecy. The matter of my brush with death seemed more dramatic than fearful, but the comment he made about my eyes worried me. I asked Jokorda how the old priest arrived at these conclusions, part of which could have been good guesswork but some of which would appear—if it were borne out by facts of the future—to be actual prophecy.

He said the Balinese priests believe in the powers of clairvoyance and prophecy. They base it on *sakti,* which is a kind

of power, or sixth sense, developed from the "charges" within
the human soul or mind. This *sakti* exists in most people,
but only a priest knows what to do with it. It is somewhat
similar to the Hindu *karma,* or the supply of good fortune
which exists for each person, but is only brought into effective realization by individual behavior. In some respects,
it is like the "luck" believed in by many people of Western
civilizations. When a man has "strong *sakti*" he has a lot of
good luck; when his *sakti* is "weak," he can expect bad fortune and even dire things to happen, such as sickness and
accidents. The old priest merely had access to my supply of
sakti, according to Jokorda; and through his clairvoyance he
read into it the things that might befall me.

It was some time after I left Bali that I returned to Philadelphia; and one of my first tasks was to move my furniture
out of storage into my new apartment. This reminded me of
the old priest's prophecy.   .

One Saturday night—almost a year after I had met the old
priest—I went to a party of old friends. I had been working
long hours, and felt more than ordinarily tired. The party
lasted until well into the morning, and when I awakened
the next day in my apartment, the room was a vague blur.

I telephoned an occulist, and he came to my apartment.
After examining my eyes, he gave me injections, and by mid-
afternoon my vision began to return. The physician who
treated me said the partial and temporary blindness was due
to overwork and stimulation. I have taken care of my eyes
since then, and the trouble has not returned.

Later that year, I again left for the Pacific. On a flight to
Hawaii we had crossed the ocean and were making our approach to the International Airport north of Honolulu,
when the plane suddenly levelled off and began to climb.

Members of the crew came back into the cabin, and there

was some hurried consultation, which worried most of the passengers. The plane circled above the broad yellow strips of the airport for about forty-five minutes; and finally the Captain gave us an explanation of what caused the delay.

The left wheel had failed to come down and lock successfully, and it had to be brought down manually. The instruments still did not show that it had locked, but the Captain had decided that he would make the attempt to land. Everything was lashed down, and we swept past a row of fire trucks and crash crews and came to a stop.

It is anybody's guess whether this was the close brush with death the old man had predicted. Since I was the party most directly concerned, I am glad he did not predict anything worse.

However, my experiences with the Javanese *dukun* and the Balinese priest—both representing a more sophisticated class of witch doctors than those of West Africa and the Amazon —stretched my imagination. Perhaps the most valid explanation was offered by Dr. Geoffrey Gorer, an English anthropologist, who had made personal observations in West Africa and also in Indonesia. Dr. Gorer spent some time in Bali just before World War II, and he was less concerned with what the Balinese believe *sakti* to be than with what *he* thinks it actually is.

In West Africa Dr. Gorer observed certain practices and rituals quite similar to those I saw at Dahomey and in the Gabun country. He admits his scientific orthodoxy was considerably shaken by some of the things he witnessed. But in Bali he was able to observe the basic development of these mystic practices by an intelligent and articulate priesthood. He compares *sakti* with musical ability. Every man has latent musical capacity, even those who appear to be "tone deaf." This capacity is not evenly divided, and it can be developed

or increased; but occasionally a genius is born with a seemingly innate knowledge of music.

Dr. Gorer has described what the Balinese call *sakti* as
"mental energy" or "mystical energy." He admits the theory
is "unscientific and irrational;" and he rests his case purely
on his own observation. He particularly calls attention to
the instructions which priests of almost every Asiatic religion
as well as of many others give to devotees and initiates, explaining how the capacity for super-sensory prescience and
clairvoyance may be developed.

Among those instructions there is invariably one: the novitiate must *believe* such a thing to be desirable, as well as
possible. This is a peculiar condition; and Dr. Gorer believes
it is indispensable for those who practice mystical powers—
including, of course, the witch doctor. Dr. Gorer says:

"The most generally granted functions (i.e., of mental or
mystical energy) are clairvoyance and telepathy, the ability to
read thoughts or see objects at a distance either in space or
time . . . Adepts are also apparently able to influence objects
at a distance without any palpable means . . . They are also
able to communicate their force to others by direct contact,
to strengthen and heal them."

Admitting that this "force" is less cultivated at present in
Western Europe and America than anywhere else in the
world, Dr. Gorer adds:

"I refuse to believe that the greater part of the world, not
only today but through all recorded history, has been engaged in rituals and practices that have given absolutely no
result."

14

In my progress down the Sunda Archipelago, that string of
islands that extends from the southeastern tip of Asia to the
aboriginal lands of New Guinea and Australia I was offered
some of the best glimpses of the inner mysteries of witchcraft.

At Surabaya, on the northeast side of the Javanese coast, I
met a Dutch resident of the city, Mr. Caals, who became
quite interested in my inquiries into the native medical
practice.

"Our greatest problem is to find some common ground
between the old customs and our newer methods of living,"
he said. "It is very difficult to make the native people believe
in modern medicine. They will trust the *dukun,* even when
they are going to die from his treatments."

He told of a foreman in his plant in Surabaya, whose son
had typhoid fever. Mr. Caals went to the home to find out
if anything could be done for the boy, and found the father,
tucked in bed with his son, trying to force rice down the
boy's throat.

"The *dukuns* have taught them that rice carries the spirit of life, which it does to a great extent. Therefore if you stuff rice into a patient, he will live. In this case, of course, the digestive tract was completely clogged."

Mr. Caals warned the father that his son would die if any food were given him until a doctor had administered certain medicines. Then he went to get a doctor. When he returned, the family *dukun* was at the boy's bedside, and soon another came to assist him.

"They spit some kind of stuff all over the boy," he said. "It was a frightful thing to see—the boy dying of fever, and the *dukuns* practicing this kind of 'medicine.' I shoved them aside and picked up the boy and carried him to a hospital. I had to place a guard in the hospital room to keep the *dukuns* and relatives out of the room. However the next day a score of relatives came to the hospital and took the boy. There was nothing the hospital attendants could do to stop it."

"What happened to the boy?" I asked.

Mr. Caals shrugged.

"They took him back home. The next day the father told me at the plant that he had gotten two bowls of rice down the boy's throat. I told him he was a fool—that the boy would die."

"Did he?" I asked.

Mr. Caals nodded. "He died—and they blamed me for it. They still think I killed the boy with white man's magic."

I thought of Pat Putnam, "Doctor Totoride," and the great gap, which he tried to bridge between the thinking of the white man and that of the native practitioner. Some of the so-called "cures" I had seen were medical monstrosities. Yet some of them worked. Of one thing I was increasingly certain: There was more in the practices than mere ignorance. As Dr. Gorer had remarked, it is not possible that so many of these practices could have gone on for centuries, with no results. The death of the boy from the forced feeding of rice may have been a medical mistake, but behind this treatment there probably existed remnants of an ancient knowledge, garbled in its transmissions through the centuries and distorted in this present-day context, but conceivably adequate in other cases.

The one indestructible element in these centuries-old practices is the element of faith. Faith existed among the Camayuras and the Jívaro head hunters of the Upper Amazon country; it was the basis of the remarkable powers of Lusungu and the fetish priests of Dahomey; it seemed to be the *sine qua non* of witch doctors everywhere.

The old Balinese priest, Ida Bagus Gede Agung, had told me that after studying with the Dutch physicians, he became quite friendly with two white physicians on Bali, and they left him some medicine, including iodine and atabrine. He said he had used these in treating his people for infected wounds and for malaria, but they were of little value since he did not have faith in them. However, when he accompanied the medication with approved rituals and incantations, and went into a trance, they were remarkably effective.

This, of course, is an unprovable point; yet I was convinced the old man believed what he was saying. I asked him, for example, how he cured a fever, and he replied, through Jokorda's translation:

"It depends upon many things—the age, sex and personality of the sick person. I feel their temperature, observe the expressions of their faces, and for different ages and sexes I prescribe different treatment, after consulting Lontar." This is the sacred medical book of Hindu priests.

In the case of catarrh, old Agung told me, his most effective remedy was hot coals mixed with chopped onions, oil of anise, salt and leaves and bark of the Dadap tree. When there was a malarial involvement, he used atabrine given him by the Dutch doctors, but only after the pills had been rubbed with Dadap bark.

Skin rashes and eruptions were often cured with lemon juice, nutmeg and Dadap bark, mixed with salicylic alcohol. A toothache could be cured with a paste made of oil from limes, two or three roots native to Bali, and ground cucumber peel. "If the patient waits too long, I have to take the tooth out," he admitted. "I do this with a screw driver and a pair of pincers."

Headaches were treated with a mixture of ground bedbugs, ginger and cow dung. In each case, certain amulets were used, some made of black coral and others of old coins.

All these were "right" or *penengens* healing. When anyone wanted an enemy destroyed, or the name of his wife's lover disclosed, Agung would send him to a "left" practitioner, who would usually achieve results without the aid of drugs, using amulets and incense to make contact with the spirits.

If this appears to be simply a low form of quackery, one has only to examine the characteristics of these drugs and healing medicines. Few of the drugs have any real curative characteristics, and fortunately most are completely harmless as well as useless.

The old priest wore his fingernails about three inches long, and he also wore two cat's-eye rings on the index finger of his right hand. This, he explained, was very powerful in warding off the influence of rival witch doctors who would try to undermine his influence with his clientele.

I asked Jokorda's uncle what he did in the case of insanity or mental derangement. He cited the case of his own sister's daughter, who had become insane when her lover married another woman. Agung had taken her to a graveyard, where there was a small shrine, and he had lighted a fire at the altar. After he had placed certain offerings before the fire, Agung and the other relatives who accompanied them to the graveyard left quietly, leaving her alone in the graveyard.

"This was more than suggestion," Jokorda explained, translating his uncle's words. "It was to show the girl that there were spirits much more powerful than herself. The shock she felt finding herself alone in this dreadful spot brought her around to her normal senses. She is now quite well and is attending a school in Singoraja."

One of the obvious functions of a witch doctor is to promote the interests of the lovelorn—either to develop interest on the part of a potential love target, or to restore the fires of passion when they have died out. Jokorda's uncle had one treatment for both situations: a betel nut, immersed in a special solution of oils. This was to be sent to the object of the unrequited affections. Once the intended victim put the betel nut in his mouth, he would be smitten with love for the witch doctor's client.

One of the prerequisites for this kind of treatment is that the victim must know that she or he is being victimized. This information is passed around readily by word of mouth. Old Ida Bagus Gede Agung admitted that the fear of a curse suggested by the machinations of a witch doctor is enough to cause most girls to revive their love for a rejected suitor rather than risk the effect of the "magic." This, probably more than the betel nut with the special oils, is what restores the fires of love.

The psychological aspects of this kind of practice are too obvious to require much emphasis. However, there are some variations in techniques that do not fit very neatly into the usual pattern. I was introduced to another priest, Gede Swanda, one of the most famous of Balinese clairvoyants. He used a pair of small green dice in order to read the future and advise his clients. I was never able to determine whether some psychological device was employed in the use of dice, or whether it was pure hokum; and for that matter, I never found out whether any of his prophecies came true.

The power of suggestion is probably the most effective tool of the witch doctor; just as it is likewise one of the most effective psychological devices used in the practice of modern medicine. One psychological device not usually associated with medicine is the dance—and in Bali and other places from the Far East to Oceania I had an opportunity to witness some of the ways in which the dance is fitted into the ritualistic and artistic pattern of the witch doctor's practice.

Probably the most pronounced form of dancing as a psychological purgative is the so-called "possession dance." This term is usually supplied to African dances, such as the "jackal dance." However, it is evident to anyone who has watched the various versions of the dance—from the most primitive to the most artistically mature—that it often serves similar purposes in different places.

When the choreography and music is developed under the watchful eye of a priest or witch doctor, or led by him, it becomes evident that the ritual or expression of the dance itself is controlled by the priest or witch doctor. If the purpose of that control is to drive out "spirits," the dance will function as a psychological purgative. One result of these "possession dances" is that the individual is "cured" of his trouble and resumes normal living.

This kind of psychological purgative has some of the basic ingredients of modern psychotherapy. The difference between the primitive and the civilized procedure is in the actual means of release. The inner needs or desires are channelled, in primitive societies, through a form of expression

that is communal, and thus the feeling of queerness and
separation from society is removed. By taking these cures in
public, the patient resolves his inner dilemma and frees himself from the control of a "spirit."

In the "Taro cult" in Papua, with which I became acquainted during several visits to New Guinea, there is a
similar but more controlled release of inner desires. The
person seeking to become a member of the cult usually has
had "dreams," which may be hallucinations. The new initiate is trained in the proper methods of dreaming, which is a
form of communication with the spirit that is seeking to
possess him. This is often referred to as *Orakaiva* magic.

The devotees of this *Orakaiva* magic believe firmly that
their dreams are real, and often prophetic. As a result, they
seek proudly to tell about their dreams, and thus a disciple
of this "dream cult" becomes a person of new importance in
his village. Often these dreams are so similar among different
members of the cult that it is impossible to tell which experiences were actual dreams, and which were versions of
dreams that were experienced by others.

When the "Taro cult" devotees get together, they sing
and beat drums, and finally dance. These dances are known
among the local Papuans as *kasamba* and they differ from
the native "sing-sing" in the frenzy and excess of emotion
that is worked up.

The guests are greeted with characteristic shouts—"Oroda!
Oroda!"—a kind of password among men of the "Taro cult."
The tempo picks up as newcomers arrive, and the young
men vie with each other in losing control of themselves.
They brandish weapons, rip down branches of banana trees
and coconut palms, and chew betel nut until the dark red
juice drips from their mouths.

The most frenzied and fantastic dance I have ever seen was

in Bali, near the town of Klungklung. This was known as
the "Kris Dance" because the dancers in frenzy literally im-
paled themselves on their sharp *kris,* or swords.

I had been traveling through the northern part of the
island when I heard that such a dance was in progress. They
often last for several days, and I made arrangements to visit
the place. As we approached the town, we had to move aside
from the road to let a long procession of men and women,
dressed in bright colored attire, pass our party. My guide
informed me that these people were going to the village of
Pak Sebali, where the Kris Dance was in progress.

I joined the procession, following an uphill trail for about
two miles; and here I came out upon a plateau at the sum-
mit of the hill. It was a pleasant landscape, covered with rice
paddies terraced along the side of the hill, with coconut groves
and gardens. On the plateau there was a temple made of
lava rock and sun-baked bricks. A large courtyard surrounded the front of the temple, closed by a low mud wall.
Banners streamed from the spear-like pinnacles of the temple
roof, and the entire place had the air of a festival.

We approached the temple, and saw great tables in the
courtyard, piled with mounds of food—cakes and bizarre
delicacies, arranged in intricate patterns on the tables. There
was a sound of music, light and tinkling; and from a gate at
the front of the temple emerged a man, carrying a white umbrella on the end of a ten-foot pole.

A group of musicians came out of the temple, and then a
column of about fifty girls streamed out, all wearing huge
headdresses made of floral pieces. This procession went out
through the courtyard gate and down a pathway, which led
to a river at the foot of the hill. I learned from my guide
that this was the beginning of the ceremony, and that the

temple gods would be brought back from the river by a group of "specially selected men."

The theory of this dance, as I learned later, was that at a certain time during the waning of the moon at the beginning of the New Year, the gods may occupy the bodies of devotees of the cult. During this period the entire population of the village may easily imagine itself individually to be possessed by gods. There have been occasions when an entire village has gone into a collective trance during these ceremonies.

I was startled when I saw the procession of "selected men" suddenly come into view, marching up the pathway where the girls had gone down. They were moving rhythmically, chanting as they advanced step by step; yet there was something unsteady, and even unwieldy about the procession. I saw that the eyes of the men were wide open and staring, as if they had lost the power of closing their eyes. They seemed to be in a state of trance.

Every now and then one of the men would turn partly to one side, and place the sharp point of a *kris* against his chest. At times they would put the other end on the ground, making a complete turn with the point of the sword on the chest. By the time the procession reached the gateway to the temple courtyard, I could see that many were bleeding from wounds in the chest, but they seemed to be completely oblivious to this.

Immediately behind the men were litters, in the form of troughs, about six feet long and two feet across. These were covered with straw and carried on long bamboo poles to which the carriers were harnessed, in front and behind the litters. In each of these litters was a god, contained in a small casket-like house.

As the procession entered the courtyard, I saw how greatly

the emotional reactions of the men and the women in the audience had increased in feverishness and intensity. The faces were strained, and a few of the spectators even lurched toward the procession, but were drawn back into the crowd. Meanwhile the men in the procession began to swerve around in the courtyard, and the litter carriers would suddenly drive with their long poles toward the crowd.

I had found a place on the mud wall to watch the procession, but the pandemonium and confusion was so great that I could make out little of what was going on. In my effort to get a better view I pushed forward, and suddenly tumbled off the wall into the courtyard.

By this time the litters and their carriers were swerving through the courtyard in erratic courses, apparently out of control, and the women in the crowd were letting out piercing shrieks. It seemed to me that the gods in the litters must be hurled into the crowd, but they had apparently been fastened down, and although they bobbed around like small craft in a stormy sea, they stayed on their moorings.

The gate to the temple had become a hopeless jam of people trying to get through. Men fell down and were literally trampled by the others. How many were maimed or killed I do not know, but the casualties must have been high. As each litter, with the long poles protruding, shot through the massed flesh into the temple, I could hear the agonized screams of the injured, many of them women.

The selected guard of honor for the gods was by this time in a state of complete frenzy. The men whirled about, stabbing at each other and at spectators with their swords. Many of them continued to make the strange pirouette around with their *kris,* with the hilt planted in the ground and the point against the chest of the dancer.

Within a few minutes the procession had been swallowed

into the inner sanctum of the temple. A few bleeding honor guardsmen were being led away by attendants, and those who lay on the ground were sprinkled with some kind of holy water which the attendants carried in gourds. The music, which had risen to a crescendo of beating drum and shrill trumpets, continued in a steady, discordant blare for some time.

The *kris* bearers who were able to walk staggered toward the temple, and others were helped by attendants. Some had to be carried into the temple. It had grown dark by the time the last of the devotees had entered the temple, and I had become so emotionally exhausted by the exhibition that I signalled my guide and we departed silently.

There is no way of analyzing this kind of ceremony, either as to its full meaning to or its emotional values for the participants. Only those who took part could possibly have any complete understanding of their own motives or reactions. But I was told by friends in Bali, who had some real knowledge of the place, that there was very little insanity in Bali, and these dances were the reason for it. How true this is I do not know; but I should think that one session of the Kris Dance would either cure or kill anyone afflicted with anxieties or neuroses. It almost did as much for me, and I was a complete onlooker.

15

In 1953 I turned southward from Bali and Borneo to New Guinea—partly because I had an invitation from the government to visit New Guinea and complete some anthropological work I had in mind for some time on the aborigines of that country; and partly out of sheer curiosity. I had been told by friends in New York that in New Guinea I would find the most elemental forms of witchcraft and "black magic" to be encountered anywhere in the world.

This proved to be very true. It was here that I found perhaps the strangest of all the adventures I have had with witch doctors and witchcraft.

The beginning of that adventure was an event known widely in jungle circles as the "Telefomin incident"—a case that is as notorious within the limited orbit of Australasian affairs as the Dreyfus case was to all the Western world. The details of the case are spread officially on the records of the Australian Mandate courts; but I had the luck to be near there when it happened, and therefore I will present my personal account, which differs in some respects from the official story, for reasons that will become obvious.

The Telefomin country lies at the headwaters of the Sepik River, among the jagged contours of mountains that raise their bony shoulders up toward the jutting peaks of the Owen Stanley Range, towering some thirteen thousand feet into a murky and often sulphurous tropical sky. This was not far from the tortuous trail over which the Japanese crawled in September 1943, when they descended upon the southern slopes of the island to within a dozen miles of Port Moresby. On the northern side, flat against the Bismarck Sea, lie the battle grounds of Buna where the Japanese forward thrust was stopped and the Pacific War turned back by Australian and American troops under General MacArthur.

My visit was a decade afterwards, and there was no trace of battle left in Wewak or its environs. However, some background of the war period in this area is necessary to make the Telefomin incident intelligible.

In 1942 the Australians had penetrated from Wewak some distance into the jungle, setting up constabulary posts on the fringe of the great plateau inhabited by head-hunting natives. Here some of the wildest and fiercest tribes in New Guinea had lived for centuries, constantly warring with each other and constantly acquiring the heads of their neighbors as proof of their superior fighting powers.

In the spring of 1942 George Ellis, assistant district officer at Angormam, together with Jim Taylor of Aitape and J. G. Jones of Wewak—all of the Australian Constabulary Forces— had moved into the upper part of the Sepik to set up posts, when the Australian Government, fearful of the onward rush of the Japanese, ordered most of its Constabulary Force to leave the island.

They had a disagreement among themselves over these orders, and in the ensuing wrangle some of the native constabulary troops turned on them and shot their officers.

This event seemed to have left a lasting impression on many of the native tribesmen, and following the end of the New Guinea campaign, when the Australian and American troops moved westward toward Biak, Morotai and the Philippines, the Australian Constabulary found it difficult to reorganize their Papuan patrols.

The tribes in the Sepik district were particularly hard to control, and many native patrols traveling along the thin trails that wound through the jungles, fell victim to the "bête men" of the Telefomin tribes.

These "bête men" were peculiar to the natives of this region. They were jungle guerillas, who would stealthily follow the patrol troopers through the forest, and dart out upon them with deadly effect. Their technique consisted of slashing at the tendon of the patrol trooper's leg. With this severed, the trooper had great difficulty traveling, and when he finally dragged himself back to the post, he was useless for patrol duty.

Somehow the tribesmen reasoned that this kind of attack would be less likely to bring reprisals than outright killing. However, murder was by no means barred from their repertoire—as the Telefomin incident will show.

During the years after the New Guinea campaign, an intensive effort was made by the Australian Constabulary Forces to organize and control the Sepik region. The natives of this area are stone-age savages, constantly engaged in inter-tribal warfare; and most of them would as soon fight as eat—and their appetites include cannibalism!

The area reeks of black magic and witchcraft. Every native lives in constant dread of being bewitched by a sorcerer, and the witch doctors are by far the most prosperous of any in the New Guinea tribes I saw during my travels.

Their religion is based chiefly on the worship of the dead. The "spirits" they fear are all "souls" of the dead, which may hover over the living, bringing all manner of evil and trouble unless they are properly propitiated or otherwise dealt with by the witch doctors. They believe—as do the natives of Africa and South America—that the spirit, or soul can leave the body, and does during sleep; and that death occurs when the spirit leaves its corporeal home permanently.

For this reason the witch doctors, who alone are able to influence and sometimes control the activities of these spirits, are feared and respected; and as the Telefomin incident disclosed to me, this fear can supersede any other fear these people have, including the fear of death itself.

Most of the native rites are involved with some phase of worship of the dead; and sacrifices of pigs—and among many tribes the "long pig," or human victim—are frequently used to propitiate the dead spirits, or *minman*.

In one example of sorcery I witnessed in the village of Wabag, near the Sepik area, a witch doctor was accused by the Constabulary patrol of "murdering" another man because he was known to have stolen a betel nut from the victim's nut bag, taking a nut that had already been bitten by the deceased. He had wrapped the chewed remains of the nut in a parcel of dry leaves, and sprinkled it with some powdered leaves, supposedly containing specific magical powers. The witch doctor then summoned the friends of the victim and announced his death—and within a few days the man died.

I never found out what punishment was meted out to the witch doctor, but it was my impression from what I was told by the native troopers at the Wabag patrol station that some

reparation was extracted by relatives of the deceased for the
loss of their kin, and the incident was then forgotten.

A few years before the Telefomin incident occurred, the
Australians had established a patrol station in the mountain-
ous area near the Papuan border, and had sought to reduce
the resistance of the Telefomin tribesmen by slow pene-
tration. Native patrols with carriers were sent through the
region, led by the two white officers assigned to the area.

The two officers in charge of the Telefomin patrol were
Patrol Officer Gerald Czarka and Cadet Patrol Officer Geoffrey Harris. Two native sub-officers, Constables Buritori and
Purari, were also stationed at the post. There was also a
Protestant missionary, a medical attendant and a geologist.
These five white people were the world's total population of
whites, as far as the Telefomin natives were concerned.
Consequently, when the Constabulary patrols began to inter-
fere with their head-hunting excursions, even arresting certain of the natives who were known to have violated the
strictures against this illegal jungle sport, the tribal chiefs
decided to eliminate the five white men and thus remove the
strange curse of law and order.

The "bête men" began to cover the patrol trails with increased activity, cutting down the runners and carriers with
a quick slash of the leg tendons. Apparently they also gave
some lethal drug to the victims, because when they returned
they were unable to remember who had attacked them—and
thus there was no evidence upon which the Australians could
arrest any native suspects.

The incident which set off the rebellion of the natives was
an accident among a group of native carriers, who had been
brought down from the mountain tribes and impressed into
service for the Constabulary Forces. While patrolling along
the Strickland River, several fell or were thrown into the

river, and many of them drowned. This incensed the tribes from which they came, who attributed this to the evil of white men's law.

The resentment of the natives was increased when their women began to ridicule the young men for failing to bring back the heads of their enemies. This custom had been pretty well discouraged by the Australian Constabulary patrols during the years of the New Guinea campaign and immediately afterwards; and the elders of the tribes became disgusted with the lack of the head-hunting spirit among the younger generation.

The old women began to tell the younger girls that the current crop of men were afraid to go into battle and kill their enemies, and that few of them ever returned with a head as a trophy. It was not long before the fear of ridicule by the women, and possibly some denial of their companionship, outweighed the fear of punishment by the Australian patrols.

The tribal chiefs in the Sepik district sent runners down to the Constabulary posts at Wabag and Wewak and asked the white people to send up goods for trading. Believing this to be an indication that the natives were submitting to organization and control, Patrol Officer Szarka and Cadet Patrol Officer Harris were sent with eight armed native patrolmen and eighty carriers. The announced objective of the trip was to complete a census of the area, but actually they were assigned to feel out the temper of the natives.

Half-way up to the Sepik area, the two officers split their forces as a precautionary move. Szarka took half the constables and some of the carriers and followed one side of a long, rugged ridge which divided the Sepik area, and Harris took the rest of the armed patrolmen and carriers up the other side to establish a camp, where Szarka would join him later.

One purpose of this maneuver was to permit the natives to see the deployment of forces, and be more impressed by the strength of two patrols than one. Once they joined again, on the lower base of a plateau which extended deep into the mountains, they would have a better knowledge of the area and the problems of terrain that confronted them in the event of a skirmish.

Harris had established his camp near a village called Terrap-davip. His men had stacked their rifles and were setting up tents for the night, when a swarm of natives came pouring down the ridge from where they had apparently been concealed above the patrol. Harris was struck with eleven arrows and a hatchet had been driven into the back of his skull. He apparently had continued to shoot, even while dying, because his gun was later found to be empty.

The constables were struck with arrows on the first charge, but managed to get to their guns and shot several of the natives before they finally were overpowered. Many of the carriers fled, and one constable escaped. He made his way across the ridge to find Szarka's patrol. He found them—all dead, with Szarka's body hacked and mangled.

Later the man who escaped made his way down to the lower base at Daru, and reported the grisly fate of the two Patrol Officers and their men. I was at Wabag, a few miles away, and I came over with members of the Constabulary Force when the ambush and massacre was reported. Later I talked with the native patrolman who had survived the attack.

A force of armed constables, led by four district officers with more than a hundred carriers was dispatched on a punitive expedition. When they reached the mountain area where the warlike Telefomin tribes lived, the natives were

astonished at the arrival of the additional white men. They
had thought that the only white men left in the world, after
the killing of the two patrol officers, were the three non-
fighting men they had previously seen in the area.

When the native scouts saw the large forces, led by the
four white officers, they raced back to the villages, and in a
short time the villages were abandoned. The Constabulary
patrols hid in the bushes until the natives returned, and then
they seized them one by one as they returned. More than a
hundred natives were arrested and taken down to Wewak
for trial.

The presiding judge was a huge, white-haired magistrate
named Ralph Gore, who had been in Papua for years. He
ruled the court with sober and dignified mien, and his
monumental figure impressed and awed the natives. Yet a
strange situation soon became evident in the trial. There
seemed to be a conspiracy of complete silence. None of the
witnesses among the native carriers would give any helpful
information; and even the man who had escaped the massacre refused to give testimony.

There were several *puri-puri* men, or witch doctors, in the
group attending the trial; and it was obvious that these men,
merely by their presence, had created an element of fear
among the natives that was more powerful than anything
Judge Gore could offer in the way of threats or intimidation.
The witnesses simply refused to talk; or they deliberately
lied, when it was quite obvious that they were lying.

Several witnesses were put into jail for refusing to testify
or for lying, and they accepted this punishment cheerfully.
One of the imprisoned witnesses told the Government interpreter, who had spent many years in New Guinea, that the
puri-puri man was "stronger" than Judge Gore or the Government. Besides, they got food in jail without working for

it, so they were content to stay there as long as the Government wished to keep them.

There were four of these trials, dragging over a year. Thirty-three men were finally convicted of complicity in the killing of the white patrol officers and native constables and carriers.

By the laws of the United Nations mandate under which Papuan New Guinea is controlled, a death sentence could not have been ordered, and no fear of this punishment could have existed among the natives. Nevertheless, the entire group of defendants and witnesses were under the grip of a compulsion more effective than all the laws and regulations propounded by the Mandate Government.

Two years after my first visit to New Guinea, I returned again to the Sepik district. On my journey I visited Rabaul, and found there an old friend, Eric Robinson, who was known throughout New Guinea as "Sepik Robbie." He was radio officer at Angoram, and had made the trip to Rabaul with his "number one boy," Pukka.

One evening when Robbie was in the Rabaul Club, Pukka came into the club looking for him in a state of excitement. He said his brother had "just killed Massa Green."

"Massa" Green was District Officer at Angoram, which was five days away by any form of communication except radio—and Pukka would have had no access to a radio. Nevertheless, he insisted his brother had killed the District Officer, and had done it with Green's rifle.

Sepik Robbie made several inquiries, but no one in Rabaul knew anything of this incident. A friend of Robinson was with him the evening the boy came into the Rabaul Club, and he told Robinson: "Regardless of the truth of what Pukka told you, I am sure he believed it. I think you ought to do something about it."

About a week later Robinson returned to Angoram, and found Green's body lying in his hut. He had been killed with his own rifle; and since no one had visited the hut in the meantime, there had been no report of the killing.

One part of the story dumbfounded me, when I was given the details by the friend of Robbie's who had been with him in Rabaul. The boy, Pukka, had insisted that his brother was "hiding in tree," and when Robinson returned to Angoram and found Green, he began to search the nearby area for some evidence of how the killing had occurred.

The brother, who had been employed at the patrol station, was found hanging by one foot high in the branches of a tree near the District Officer's hut. His foot had become entangled with some twisting vines and he apparently had fallen, and hung there in the tree until he died.

The most astonishing part of the story, which I got first-hand from Sepik Robbie and his friend, was that the boy, Pukka, could remember nothing of what he had told Robbie that night at the Rabaul Club. And yet the two men listened to his story of a murder several hundred miles away—which no one in Rabaul could have known about at the time!

Later I returned to the Sepik River country, near the place where the Telefomin massacre had occurred. I approached the village of Tambunum in a dugout with a patrol officer, and a party consisting of two carriers and eight native constables. We were well armed, since this was the area where there had been so much unrest a few years earlier.

As we headed inshore, I noticed heavy storm clouds gathering above us. The thick clouds were rolling through the mountain gorges, and the sky was becoming overcast and leaden, the rain clouds swept along on heavy winds in the upper air.

As we approached the shore, a runner for the native chief

paddled out to our boat and told us, by words and gestures, that we would not be allowed to land. It was evident that some crisis had occurred, or was occurring in the village.

"They believe we are bringing rain," the patrol officer said. "Their big sing-sing takes place at this time of the year, and they do not want us to bring rain and interrupt the ceremony."

A "sing-sing" is a native ceremony, during which highly decorated warriors, painted with yellow, blue, orange and red dyes, wearing enormous head-dresses made of bird of paradise feathers, come from miles around to participate in the feast and rituals. Various forms of possession dances take place, each cult trying to outdo the others in the variety and splendor of their performance.

One of my reasons for coming upriver was to take pictures of this particular "sing-sing"—and also to take some casts and measurements of the heads and faces of the natives for my anthropological studies.

I glanced at the sky, and it looked like one of those flash storms that come up suddenly in the tropics, drenching everything in their path and vanishing as swiftly as they come. I took a chance that the storm would not hit Tambunum in full force.

"Tell him I am a great witch doctor," I told one of the constables. "Tell him I have come to see the big sing-sing and that there will be no rain."

The messenger from the village seemed a bit dubious, since it had already begun to sprinkle, but he let us follow him to the chief's hut. I brought two dishpans with me, and using these as a combination of cymbals and a drum, I began to march around the chief's house, raising a terrific din with my improvised instruments.

The second time around the hut, the rain stopped. The

old chief had watched my antics with some interest, and he now summoned carriers who ran down to unload our canoes. I pressed my luck a little further by announcing to the chief that as long as I remained at the village, there would be no rain.

That night a lightning storm swept down from the hills, with a great deal of thunder and flashes of lightning; but there was no rain. The next morning it was clear and sunny —and my reputation as a weather prophet was at its highest point.

I took my pictures—about five thousand feet of film—and left for Wewak and the United States. I had planned to return the following year, but in July—just before my scheduled departure from Philadelphia—I received word that a member of my family was ill, and postponed my trip. Later when I was again about to leave, my throat became infected and so I changed my plans and went to Spain instead.

Later I learned from my friends in the District Office at Wewak that my arrival in the Sepik area would have been most unfortunate at that time. The village of Tambunum and that of a nearby tribe were at war with each other—and the "white doctor" with the "many eyes" was the cause of it all!

This seemed rather ridiculous at first; but when I got all the facts it was not so ridiculous. The people of the rival village had been about to hold a sing-sing when the rain struck at the time of my departure. The villagers whose festival had been washed out accused the people of Tambunum of having imported a "white doctor" to make *puri-puri* with the rain, since it missed Tambunum but poured watery earth upon every other village in the area.

This was not merely a violation of neighborliness; it was a form of treachery understood only by the natives, according to my informants from Wewak. The result was war; and they were still fighting at the time I planned to return.

This is not related with any idea of enhancing myself as a weather prophet—even though the Lusungu incident offers some striking evidence in this respect. It simply offers another coincidence—and among these strange peoples coincidences of this character become so commonplace that even a white visitor, like myself, begins to take them in stride.

Probably the most startling coincidence of all was that a letter had been sent to me, warning against coming back to New Guinea at this time—and it was not delivered until a month after I planned to leave.

16

---◄●●●►---

DURING MORE THAN twenty years of wandering around the
world, blessed with more curiosity than a normal man should
have, I have had many opportunities to watch a witch doctor
from a ringside seat. Some of the experiences have been
merely interesting; others have been startling, and still others
have been vaguely chilling, as if I had plucked back momen-
tarily the veil of the unknown and had glimpsed something
forbidden to civilized eyes.

The witch doctor is an economic parasite. Whatever function he performs for the tribe, it is not one of food-getting
labor. His primitive neighbors respect him and need his
services, just as we need a modern physician. The witch
doctor is paid in prestige, and with gifts of the necessaries of
life, for he is recognized by the community as necessary to
its life.

Frequently, however, he is a social or physical misfit. He
may be a weakling or a cripple, or even an epileptic. Such
was the case with Pamantauho. Frequently he is given to

dreams and trances, or other abnormal psychological states. In some tribes the word for a witch doctor is the same as the word for an insane man, since a witch doctor functions by the spirits he is able to control, and insanity is believed to be "possession" by a spirit.

The witch doctor usually acts in an advisory or consulting capacity, and seldom as an executive. Most significantly, he is invariably a shrewd psychologist. In addition, he must also be a politician and showman. He understands his audience, which expects him to entertain as well as care for his people. His job is to maintain the health, both physical and mental, of his community, and his techniques include a weird combination of natural and supernatural elements, understanding, and common sense.

He goes by different names in different places. In Africa he is a *ngombo* along the West Coast; in Central Africa he is a *nyanga,* and among the Fang nations he is a *mb'unga.* In South America he is a *curandeiro* or a *feiteceiro* among the Portuguese-speaking peoples of Brazil; and in the Peruvian Andes he is a *brujo.* In Malaya he is a *mendug,* in Borneo a *madang;* in Java a *dukun.* Among the Greenland Eskimos he is an *angakok.*

He is respected mainly because his powers are feared, but he is by no means evil. He is usually the wisest man in the village—doctor and counsellor to his patients. He possesses most of the lore and knowledge that exists in his tribe.

It is necessary in many parts of the world for a witch doctor to undergo a great deal of training as a novitiate; and indeed, there are no tribes as far as I know that do not provide some training for their future witch doctors. A few, like the Camayuras, are not particularly rigid in training, accepting slight aberrations of the mind or body as sufficient indication that the practitioner is in touch with the spirits. Most of the African tribes, however, have a severe training ritual.

In the Ubangi Valley of the Belgian Congo, at a small village called Kefusa, I once witnessed a ceremony of initiation for boys who were to become apprentices to a cult of *ngombos*. The ceremony called for great physical stamina on the part of the young novitiates. It was held early in the morning in a grove of palms, with the towering jungle behind. Two chiefs, one wearing a red coat of a U. S. Marine Officer, escorted me to the place, with two of the young candidates hopping along ahead of us. I was horrified to note that an arrow was protruding from the cheek of each boy.

The *ngombo yatseksuku,* or chief witch doctor, was carried out of the palm grove on the shoulders of two natives. There were about a dozen lesser witch doctors around him, all jumping into the air and screaming as if they had suddenly gone wild. They continued past us to a point near the edge of the village. I had observed that there were no women present; all had been confined to their huts.

The men continued to dance, forming a circle around the *ngombo.* Then the *lemba,* or headman of the village, stepped into the circle and addressed the group. He seemed to be asking questions, and a roar of voices in chorus answered him. The assembly had formed near the end of a long grass-thatched hut; and from the darkness near this hut eight boys suddenly emerged, walking single file. These were the novitiates. A fire was lighted near the entrance to the hut, and green branches thrown over it to create a great deal of smoke. The boys filed into the hut, and remained there for perhaps twenty minutes. Then they began to stagger out, coughing from the fumes and apparently on the verge of asphyxiation.

The men outside rushed at them, slapping them and driving them back into the hut as fast as they emerged, gagging in the night air. After a short time some of the men went into the hut and dragged the boys out. Most were half-conscious, but some had passed out and had to be carried over to an open place.

Four drummers, who had been beating tom-toms, lined up behind the boys and began to beat their drums harder and harder. Perhaps the incessant din awakened the boys. One by one they sat up, rubbing their eyes. As soon as they were conscious, they were driven into the hut again.

This process was repeated for a couple of hours, the boys being pushed back into the smoke-filled hut and dragged out again when they were on the point of suffocation. Finally, just at dawn, the eight boys were lined up and they began to walk down toward a river, which was about four miles distant. At the edge of the river there was a huge, conical mound; and I understood, to my horror, what this ordeal would be. The mound was a nest of wild fire-ants, each about a half-inch long. These ants are among the most vicious and ravenous insects in Africa.

Each boy was marched into the water, and a segment of the ant nest was taken out and put on the head of each boy. They were forced to hold two stones in their hands, to prevent scratching or scraping off the ants.

As soon as the ants had been turned loose on the boys, each boy was permitted to start up the river to a place where one of the witch doctors of the village was sitting under a tree. He was painted in a ghastly way with marks on his face roughly resembling the face of a crocodile; and he held a machete in each hand and an arrow between his teeth. After examining each boy, he would wave one machete at him and the boy would turn and run back down the river. Then he was allowed to jump into the water and rid himself of the ants. At the conclusion of the ceremony each boy, his face and neck swollen and disfigured from the ant bites, was given a red parakeet feather, presumably the insignia of his apprenticeship in the secret cult of witch doctors, in which he was now a member.

The ordeal of admission to these secret cults seems to have a two-fold purpose: one is to "try out" the candidate, to determine whether he will be fit to carry on the mysterious and often terrifying rituals of the craft; and the other is to impress the people of the village or tribe with the fearful powers of the witch doctor, so they will respect him.

In many instances I have seen, the ceremonies of initiation into a cult are almost childlike in character, and often are witnessed by the entire village. The Akikuyu tribes of British East Africa perform simplified rites of initiation, merely killing a goat and feeding it half-cooked to the neophytes, and then covering portions of the body of each candidate with strips of goat-skin. In other cases, the ceremony is more elaborate and is performed secretly with only members of the cult of witch doctors in attendance.

In his relations with his people, the witch doctor utilizes psychological mechanisms that antedate Freud by many hundreds, and perhaps thousands, of years. He is a precursor not only of Freud, but of Mary Baker Eddy.

The similarity of these psychological mechanisms passes beyond the boundaries of ethnic custom, of language, and even of geography. The same basic patterns of psychological knowledge may be found in one variant or another scattered around the world—among the Indian tribes of North America; in Brazil and in the Andes; in Greenland and Alaska; in Australia and New Guinea and in the South Sea Islands. Obviously, the same factors in human nature are basic to all of them.

The power of suggestion is as old as humanity. Its force

was discovered long before Mary Baker Eddy. There are examples of it in the Old and New Testaments, the Talmud and the Koran. It is not strange that the witch doctor should have used it; but what is strange is that he uses it in ways that so closely parallel the theories of modern medicine, combining the mystical elements of suggestion with such practical techniques as hypnosis and sleight-of-hand, or medically useless drugs which nevertheless give confidence, and therefore aid, to the patient.

The witch doctor often has the bedside manner of the modern doctor, not that of the old-fashioned practitioner. He does not enter a patient's hut with a funereal mien and a solemn shake of his head, or an attitude that "the patient is doing as well as can be expected." Instead of setting the stage for death, the witch doctor tries to revive his patient with optimistic prophecies—chiefly having to do with his own powers and promises of death to the patient's enemies.

Above all, he uses psychological devices. Modern psychiatry may regard the employment of mystery and reference to the unknown as basically unsound practice; yet what is the couch in the psychiatrist's office but a device for laying a foundation for dependence upon the mysterious and unknown? Once the patient is transported into a realm of his own dreams and fancies by this mental sedative, the psychological "witch doctor" of our own age is free to manipulate the confidence he has thus inspired. In this inner sanctuary of the mind he can dredge up buried treasures of memory—hopes and fears and phobias—and either free or entangle the patient in a mental net of his own weaving.

One type of ritual that the witch doctor practices is "smelling out" the source of evil. This requires a high degree of psychological skill in manipulating the mind of the victim and the customs of the tribe so that the victim readily admits

his guilt—even when he is not in reality guilty. His faith in
the witch doctor enables him to believe that a spirit has possessed him and made him guilty. The smelling out of the
source of evil is usually carried out in the presence of the
entire tribe. This reaffirms the faith of all the members of
the tribe in the powers of the witch doctor, and it provides
the psychological advantage of mass hypnosis and general
hysteria which palpably influences the attitude of the subject or patient.

The "casting of the sticks" is a favorite African method
used to smell out the cause of disease or other troubles. It is
an ancient practice, and has been forbidden by white man's
law in many parts of Africa. Yet I have seen it performed,
and to this day I have no idea how it works—except that it
does.

The practice, known as *m'tambo* among many of the Bantu
tribes, involves the throwing of a number of intricately
carved sticks, or polished bones, upon the ground, between
two lines—one white and the other red. Usually the members of the tribe squat around in a circle, while the *ngombo*
gathers his sticks, or bones. Sometimes they are fancifully
carved in the shapes of animals, and in a few tribes a rather
crude resemblance to the signs of the zodiac have been noted.
There are often heads of goats, snakes, elephants, lions, and
antelopes carved on the end of the polished stick or bone.
Each has some significance; the lion is a symbol of strength
and victory, the snake a symbol of revenge against an unknown enemy. The crocodile is almost always the symbol of
death, and is greatly feared in consequence.

The magic objects are tossed out on the ground. In the
simpler ceremonies they simply fall flat, and the direction
they point indicates the guilty persons. Several old timers
in Africa have described rituals in which the sticks or bones

actually jump around, and even rise to a vertical or semi-vertical position, similar to the rope in the "Indian rope trick." I have heard of the bones actually dancing in a macabre jungle jig, until they got themselves into position to point the finger at the guilty party.

The red and white lines are used to determine affirmative and negative answers to questions asked of the accused, or of the patient, if he is being interrogated. If the bone falls on the red line, the answer is "yes"; if it is on the white line, "no." In this way, the spirits are supposed to indicate guilt, or the source of evil.

The propitiation of spirits and the exorcism of malign spirits from the bodies of the living are natural functions of the native medicine man or witch doctor, just as the reduction of a fever or elimination of disease-causing germs is the proper function of our own medical practitioners. One primitive "theory of disease" that is prevalent throughout the American continents is that "arrows" have been "shot" by spirits or sorcerers into the ailing individual. This "arrow theory" is used by the natives to account for many events.

The nature of a pestilence which had swept certain tribes on the Xingú River but had not bothered others, was explained as follows: In the depth of night a demon comes to the door of an Indian hut and knocks, asking permission to enter. When the person who is living in the hut appears to open the door, the demon scratches him. He then flies from hut to hut, letting loose the poisons of disease with his "arrows"—fingernails—until the entire population of the village is infected.

Among certain tribes of Indians a common headache is attributed to a mystic "arrow" shot by a witch. When an Indian feels a pain in his head, particularly when there is some swelling of the eyes, he feels sure that a sorcerer has bewitched him by shooting "arrows" at him, and that these "arrows" have become imbedded in the place where he feels the pain.

When an Indian medicine man begins the process of bewitching a victim—either on his own account or for a client—he will spend several days in preparation. During this time he may abstain from sexual activities, take little or no food, and not talk with anyone. His preparations frequently are made at night. He stews up the potions with which he intends to summon the spirits and be advised by them as to what kind of "arrows" he must shoot. Often he coughs up a nasal secretion, and spits this into his hand; and then he bends over his hand, whispers the name of the Indian he plans to bewitch, and then throws the stuff away. Even the tales of the Indians reflect this theory, as the following story told me by an Indian in the Xingú country will illustrate.

The wife of a medicine man went into the field to bring some yams, and noticed a vulture flying from the south. The bird hovered over her and then alighted, and she felt a sudden pain in her chest. She was afraid she had been bewitched by an "arrow" shot by the vulture, and tried to chase the bird away; but it would fly only a short distance and then alight, looking steadily at her. Finally she ran in terror to her house, and her husband summoned another medicine man. He drank a strong drink and told her she had been bewitched by a sorcerer from another village. He tried to cure her, but she died.

There is nothing in such a story that indicates anything more than a strong imagination; yet the woman died, and everyone in her tribe was convinced she died from sorcery.

Witch doctors may perform all manner of tricks to bolster their position in the tribe. Even my friend, Pimento, was not averse to trickery. On one occasion my Indian guide was bitten by a tiny blow-fly *(Hexepod diptera hyperderma)*. The fly gets its common name from the fact that the larva, or screw worm, is hatched under the skin and forms a tiny hole in the skin through which it can breathe. The worm can become as much as a half-inch long; and since it has barbs on its coat, it is difficult to extract. If the worm is crushed, it may easily infect the area and cause blood poisoning.

The afflicted Indian became miserable as the insect grew, and finally he went to Pimento. The witch doctor was very cooperative. He simply borrowed a cigarette from me, placed a small piece of cotton over the tiny hole in the skin and blew smoke through the cotton. Then he danced around his patient for a short time, and leaned over the wound and whispered a few words.

The Indian later told me, quite proudly:

"He speak and worm hear, senhor. Believe me, worm come out!"

Obviously, Pimento had used his knowledge of the effect of nicotine on these mites to draw it out of the skin. It is a well-known remedy in places where they are found. Yet the dance and the accompanying performance convinced the man that only a witch doctor, such as Pimento, could have helped him.

17

Looking back through this personal history over the past dozen years, during which I have watched uncivilized and semi-civilized man in the jungle depths, it is impossible to avoid one rather startling conclusion: the word "coincidence" is not broad enough to encompass all these sights I have witnessed.

From the Upper Marañón to the Sepik River in New Guinea there have been too many "coincidences" to be credible. And as a final filip, I offer a snake story.

In the Spring of 1953, on my way back from New Guinea, I spent several weeks in Malaya, that feathery strip of land curling out like a "peacock's tail"—the native name by which it is known—from the bulk of Siam to the Sunda Archipelago. One evening, walking down from the Raffles Hotel in Singapore, I stopped to listen to the plaintive music of a Hindu fakir, playing a flute and chattering his pitch to the assembed crowds.

He sat cross-legged, wearing a massive yellow turban.

When I came closer, he looked at me and said in excellent English, "Are you an American, Sahib?"

I said I was. The Hindu nodded; and then he gave himself over to intense concentration upon a small basket, which lay between his crossed legs. I was sure that inside the basket was a snake, so I tossed a dollar bill at his knees, and without seeming to interrupt his concentration, he deftly covered the bill with his hand and pocketed it.

He began to play a flute, and soon the black head of a snake appeared, full of a kind of suppressed vitality, protruding from the basket. The Hindu played gently, swaying his body in rhythm with the music, and I saw that the snake, slowly shooting upward like a magically growing plant, was swaying to the same rhythm.

A voice at my ear, speaking in clipped English accents, said:

"It is queer, isn't it—seeing that the snake is deaf?"

I looked around and saw a tall, ruddy-faced man, wearing the conventional "pukka sahib" pith hat. His gray, twinkling eyes regarded me pleasantly.

"I saw you at the hotel, Doctor. You are the fellow who is interested in witch doctors?"

I indicated I was; and the man went on:

"Pardon my presumption—but I know something about snakes and it is just as well that you understand these things too. All snakes are stone deaf. They have no central organs for hearing. But they can see and feel, and the swaying of the man's body is what does it. The music is only a show."

I was surprised at this information.

"You notice that the man taps the flute constantly as he plays," the Englishman went on. "This vibration is much more important than the noise. The vibration is felt by the delicate perceptory organs of the snake, and this makes him rise out of the basket. He senses some alien object, and wants to see what it is. The swaying fascinates him, and as long as it continues, the snake will sway with the man."

My informant then introduced himself as Dr. William A. Tweedie, curator of small reptiles at the Raffles Museum; and as we returned to the hotel, he told me a great deal about snakes. Among other things, he told me that the natives of Malaya believe in the power of the hamadryad, the "King Cobra," to enter the vital organs of a human being and poison him with its venomous fangs, without any visible outward evidence of the attack.

I recalled a story I had heard from a witch doctor of the Kalopalos Indian tribe in the central Amazon, concerning the death of Col. P. H. Fawcett of the Royal English Artillery, whose disappearance in the jungles of Brazil in 1925 has been one of the most fascinating mysteries of this century. This witch doctor, who had seen Fawcett in the village where he was last reported alive, said he died "because an enemy had looked at him with a bad eye, and sent a snake into his stomach . . . And when Fawcett tried to vomit the snake from his stomach, the snake bit him and killed him." He also believed, although half-way across the world from Malaya, that a snake could enter a living man's body, like a spirit, and destroy him.

The fact that snakes are regarded by witch doctors in South America, and in some parts of Africa, as a reincarnation of the souls of dead sorcerers, is well established. The witch doctor who can control a snake has at his disposal a powerful force to assist him in his work, either for good or for evil.

While we were in the bar at the Raffles Hotel having a nightcap, a hotel attendant came in and touched my sleeve.

"Pardon, Doctor—a man in Number 14 is very sick!"

I went to my room, got my medical kit, and followed the Indian.

An old man lay on the bed. His shoes had been removed, and his shirt was open to his waist. His head was rolling from side to side, and his mouth was open, twisted with some kind of agonizing pain. He was evidently trying to speak, and I leaned over and listened. All I could hear was: "Margrit! Margrit!" Then he said very softly, "That snake— Margrit . . ."

His head rolled over, and I reached for his wrist, and then lifted his eyelids. The man was dead.

"It's Captain Gormley, sir," the attendant said. I suggested they notify the coroner, and take whatever steps were necessary to notify his relatives. After a few questions, it developed that the man had been drinking heavily, and had been seized with some kind of delirium during the evening. He had muttered the word "Margrit" and made several unintelligible references to snakes.

The following day I read in the morning newspaper the story of "Captain Nelson Gormley," retired British Army Officer, who had "dropped dead" at a local hotel. There seemed to be no direct cause of his death, and it was attributed to a "heart attack."

It was not until some weeks later that I learned the complete story of Captain Gormley. I was stopping at a rubber plantation on Java as a guest of the English manager, Mr. Philip Fletcher, whom I had met at Singapore.

We were sitting on the verandah of the plantation house when the overseer, a man named Hanman, drove up in his car and beckoned to our host. When Mr. Fletcher returned, he was visibly disturbed.

Hanman had been out on a field trip, inspecting the plantation. A noise which he described as "the call of a hamadryad" had been heard. I was surprised at this; I had never imagined a snake had a "call." Fletcher assured me that snakes could make a noise that was audible to a man.

Hanman had investigated the noise, and found two cobras draped on the branches of a tree. He had shot at one, and one of the natives, a fellow named Abdul, had warned him that if he killed the cobra, the mate of the dead snake would follow him. Hanman said he continued through the trees, walking rapidly, and the snakes had followed. Finally Abdul told him to change his direction, and the snakes would become confused and continue on the same path. Hanman swung off at a ninety degree angle, and within a short time there was no further sign of the snakes.

"We've got to get the snakes," Fletcher said. "The snake Hanman hit will be dangerous until he is killed."

"Why?" I asked.

Fletcher shrugged.

"Snakes are queer," he said. "The natives believe they are spirits of dead people—mostly dead sorcerers."

I was quite interested. I told him of the incident at the Raffles Hotel, in Singapore, in which the retired British Army Officer, Captain Gormley, had died muttering something about snakes.

"Gormley!" Fletcher exclaimed. "My God, don't tell me he was alive—a fortnight ago!"

Fletcher then told me about Captain Gormley. He had known him twenty years earlier, having served with him in the Army. Gormley had been a subaltern, stationed on Fletcher's post in Malaya. He had finally gotten leave and returned to England to get married. When he arrived back at the post, his wife was with him.

"Margrit was a lovely creature," Fletcher said. "Slender

and pretty, with a mass of fiery red hair. She had one trouble, however—she was badly afraid of snakes."

One day Gormley brought in a dead cobra he had killed outside the officers' quarters; and one of the officers decided to play a trick on Margrit Gormley. This was a young subaltern named O'Brien, Fletcher said. He persuaded Gormley to let him take the dead snake into his wife's quarters and leave it where she would find it.

"Gormley agreed, like a damned fool," Fletcher told me. "We were all sitting in the outer room when she came in and went into her bedroom. In a moment there was a scream and after a while we went into see how badly she had been frightened. Margrit was lying on the bed, and Gormley reached down and put his hand against her cheek. Then he turned toward us, and I had never seen such a terrible look on the face of any man. She was dead."

Fletcher said the originator of the practical joke, O'Brien, started to lift the body from the bed, and a snake slithered out from the woman's skirts and disappeared through the open door.

"Did you kill the snake?" I asked.

Fletcher shook his head. There was a hard twist to his mouth.

"I shot at the cobra, and nicked it in the neck," he said. "It got away."

"What happened to Gormley?" I asked.

"Cracked up. You saw what he looked like in Singapore. He'd been there for years. This was only about twenty years ago, and Gormley was a young man—but he got old pretty fast. O'Brien, the fellow who thought up the idea, is in an asylum in England."

I asked Fletcher if he had any theory as to why the cobra

crawled into the room—since they notoriously avoid human beings unless cornered or attacked.

He shook his head.

"I spoke to a native who knows about such things. He said the snake was getting revenge on Gormley for killing its mate. But how could the cobra know Gormley was married to the girl? To the natives, of course, it is all a matter of witchcraft—and spirits."

"What's your theory?" I asked.

Fletcher shrugged.

"Just a coincidence," he said.

A few days later I returned to the Raffles Hotel in Singapore. In the bar I met two English guests who had been in the hotel when Captain Gormley died. They told me of a rather strange occurrence. The Hindu boy who had called me to go up to Captain Gormley's room had found a huge cobra on the golf links. There were no marks of a snake's fangs on Captain Gormley, yet there were Indians in the hotel who believed the snake might have killed him.

I looked up Dr. Tweedie, with whom I was very eager to discuss the matter. His thin, intelligent face became tense.

"Did you say Mr. Fletcher shot the snake in the neck?"

I nodded affirmatively.

"He said he was sure he hit it from the way the snake reacted to the shot. But the snake got away."

Dr. Tweedie got up slowly, and asked me to come with him to the reptile section in the Museum. There he showed me the body of a fifteen-foot cobra.

"The Hindu boy killed it. He thought it was a python. They sell them to the Chinese to eat—supposed to make people stronger, like your goat glands. But this was a hamadryad —fifteen feet, seven inches. Largest ever found in Singapore.

The boy found it on the golf links the day after Gormley died."

He pointed to a gray scar on the neck of the dead snake. "Somebody shot this old boy—in the neck."

* * * * * *

After twenty years of wandering among the primitive practitioners of the world's oldest profession, I can only say with Shakespeare, to civilized people: "There are more things in heaven and earth, Horatio, than are dreamt of in your philosophy!"